Tom

PRO EVO

Pro Evolution – Guideline for an Age of Joy

Asama AG Publishers
CH-7001 Chur, Switzerland

The author (1911–2001) studied first agriculture and then economics. He had a successful career as a business man and business consultant. In search of the origin and meaning of existence, he discovered in the 1950's a new, simple and reliable guideline for human thought and action. This guideline is oriented on cosmic evolution. Scientists have termed it the "evolutionary ethic".

The author, beginning in 1971, published books about his discovery under his own name and pseudonyms. The titles included *Lebensrichtig, Age of Joy, On the Side of Life, Zeitalter der Freude* and *ProEvo.* The editions now available are *ProEvo* in German and this English translation of it.

2009

 For information write to: Verlag Asama AG, Postfach 22, CH-7001 Chur, Switzerland.
Printed in Germany. Cover design by Gassner & Seger AG, Vaduz, Liechtenstein.

ISBN 978-3-9522519-0-4
www.proevo.ch

Contents

Part III Examples of Applying the New Insights – Including Clarification of Questions and Enigmas that Have Long Occupied Mankind

Preface

This book sets forth a new view of the world and of life.

And it presents a new guideline for human thought and action, one which probably will be valid for all time. Through examples from all areas of existence, it shows that by thinking and acting in accordance with this new guideline we can achieve *optimal development of our personal lives and our society.*

Origin of this Book

During my professional life I took note of kinds of behavior that created joy and well-being.

Later I searched for the cause of these phenomena.

Both led to the ideas in this book

Tomotom

Part I

In Search of the Origin and Meaning of Existence

Where are we?

The Universe

The Earth, the cosmic body on which we live, is a planet of our sun. The sun is one of billions of suns in our galaxy, the Milky Way.

Our Milky Way, at its widest, has a diameter of over 900,000 trillion kilometers. Even light takes 100,000 years to cover this distance, despite its unimaginable speed of 300,000 kilometers per second. The Earth is situated approximately 250,000 trillion kilometers, or 27,000 light years, northwest of the center of the Milky Way.

All the stars in the night sky visible to the naked eye belong to our Milky Way. Yet this Milky Way makes up only a tiny part of the universe. Besides our own Milky Way there are many billions more galaxies of similar size, most of them millions of light years away from one another.

The exploration of space has only just begun. Perhaps it will soon be discovered that the universe we know today, with its diameter of 15 to 20 billion light years, is only a small part of a much more extensive world organism.

Space is infinite – large beyond the understanding of present-day man.[1] Our Earth disappears in it like a drop of water in the ocean.

---

[1] "Man" is always to be understood in its generic sense, including both woman and man, unless the context indicates otherwise.

And on this tiny speck in the immensity of the universe lives mankind.

What are we?

Prime Force – Energy

The cosmos – the whole universe, our infinitely large and varied world – evidently consists of a single building material: Prime Force, energy.[2]

All things – whether electromagnetic fields, atoms, cosmic bodies, crystals, plants, animals, people, ideas, music, etc. – are therefore *forms* of energy; and the multiplicity of forms is the result of differences in the structure and vibration of the energy in them.

Prime Force – energy – therefore forms the organism of the world. There are – in our conception – no "empty" spaces in it: it consists of forms which are perceivable by man, of forms which are so weakly or strongly concentrated, or so far away, that man cannot yet detect them, and of unstructured – formless – energy.

The infinitely large energy-organism of the cosmos is thus a *unity,* which includes everything. Nothing and no one is outside it.

---

[2] "Prime Force" and "energy" are used in this book to refer to the primary element of the universe. Great thinkers of all ages – for example, in the 20th Century *Albert Einstein* (Theory of General Relativity), *Werner Heisenberg* (Field Theory for the Structure of Elementary Particles), *Theilhard de Chardin* and *Stephen Hawking* – have supposed that the cosmos consists of a single basic element, which they called, among other things, *prime force* or *energy.*

Long before the days of modern science, particularly gifted individuals intuitively understood this. They sensed that the universe with all its forms consists of a single, uniform, building material, which they called the *One* or the *Prime Force.* Here are some examples of their insights:

Lao Tzu: "Everything consists of prime force." Confucius: "I know only one thing; that this One is everything." Hermes Trismegistos, Smaragd Tablets: "Out of the One, all things have been created, all creatures born. The One is the father of all the wonders of the world. What is above and what is below are equal." St. John the Apostle: "Everything is contained in the One." Mohammed: "Everything is You and nothing is outside of You." Japanese Buddhism: "Everything is a unity. The rose in bloom is an event in that unity, and you are an event in that unity. All things and creatures make up that unity. Every stone, every living being, is the child of that unity". Indian proverb: "The oneness sleeps in the stone, breathes in the plant, dreams in the animal and awakens in man."[3]

Already thousands of years ago, creative people intuitively knew also of unstructured energy. Unstructured, formless energy corresponds to the Chinese concept of "non-being", the idea of not being formed, and the Indian concept of "Prana", the "life-

---

[3] Esoteric thinkers throughout the ages have probably known of "the prime force of which everything consists."

force in a state of undeveloped radiance and perfect balance”.

Since the world with all its forms consists apparently of energy, we *too are forms of energy, like cells, as it were, in the energy-organism of the universe.*

How did we come into existence?

Cosmic Evolution

The early course of evolution, from unstructured energy (Prime Force) up to hydrogen in the universe, is still unclear.

According to the prevailing opinion today, the evolution of our known world began with a "Big Bang", which is supposed to have created the elementary particles out of which the hydrogen of the universe was formed. But still unanswered is the question, among others, of what could have given rise to the Big Bang. Also all other scientific theories about the beginning and first steps of evolution are unproven and incomplete. But the evolution from hydrogen up to man can already be explained and proved:

> The hydrogen in the universe condenses into clouds and later into stars. In the course of time there occur on these hydrogen stars, through rising internal pressure and resulting heat, nuclear reactions among hydrogen atoms, through which other atoms and molecules are formed.
>
> When these stars begin to cool and environmental conditions are appropriate, severe thunderstorms take place constantly on them. Through the effect of the lightning on hydrogen, ammonia and methane, amino acids arise. These acids lead to the formation of proteins, which are the basis for the development of plant and animal life.

These processes of change in their various stages – from hydrogen to proteins – can for the most part already be reproduced in the laboratory.

The course of evolution from hydrogen masses to proteins is thus researched and provable, as is the further evolution on Earth which took place in the following stages:

From proteins one-celled organisms evolved. From these evolved two-layered metazoic organisms, three-layered structures which formed many organ systems (such as the central nervous system with simple brain), the chordate organisms with chorda and gill systems, vertebrates without jaw or limbs, fish, amphibians, reptiles, primitive insect-eating mammals, half-apes, apes with better sight and stronger drive for exploration of surroundings, higher apes, primates, and finally man with advanced brain and speech. (From J. Huxley)

We still do not know very much about the course of evolution on other cosmic bodies. But since they all – like Earth – consist of energy, the same or similar forms would have evolved as on Earth, if the same or similar environmental conditions prevailed.

If environmental conditions on other cosmic bodies differ from those on Earth, then evolutionary forms different from those on Earth will have developed there.

But on all cosmic bodies where temperature and pressure conditions permit the formation of large molecules – even if the other environmental factors are totally different from those on Earth – energy will continue to evolve and finally become conscious of itself.[4]

The most highly evolved energy form we know of is man. In him the capacity for thought and consciousness is the furthest developed.

In space there are many billions of cosmic bodies with the same or similar environmental conditions as on Earth. In addition, there are many more billions with probably entirely different environmental conditions from those on Earth, but on which still the building of large molecules – and therefore of highly complex forms of concentrated energy – is possible.

Presumably on countless of these billions of cosmic bodies energy forms have been able to develop which have reached the same or a similar level of consciousness as man. On cosmic bodies on which more favorable environmental conditions, or similar but longer lasting ones, than on Earth prevailed, probably energy forms have evolved which surpass man in intelligence and consciousness.

---

[4] In accordance with Theilhard de Chardin.

Are we a product of chance?

All forms of energy known to us are continuously changing. But this constant change does not happen chaotically. It is an *evolution* which produces ever more concentrated and complex energy forms with more and higher capabilities.

The process of change of the energy forms known to us tends – as a whole – in the same direction. Even those forms which appear to remain constant or which arise out of the disintegration of other energy forms are always again being incorporated anew in the evolution toward more intensive and more complex energy concentrations.

How can this constant change, this unstoppable *tendency,* be explained? How was it initiated, aroused? How is it kept going?

Scientific opinion today is approximately as follows:

> The evolution of our world from the beginning up to man took place *through chance*: the evolution of matter in a "self-organization through natural laws", and the biological evolution in a "self organization of life".[5]

---

[5] When unstructured energy first changes from its state of rest and equilibrium, evolution begins, life starts, becomes *living.* Therefore not only the biological evolution but also the evolution of matter should be called *life.* The terms *evolution* and *life,* as used in this book, have like meanings.

Some scientists believe that the evolution of matter and the biological evolution up to man have been a *uniquely favorable result of chance*, that is against all probability and therefore cannot be repeated in the universe even a second time, let alone more often.

Probably the majority of scientists are of the opinion that the chance events necessary for evolution occur wherever the requisite environmental conditions last *long enough*; and that therefore a same or similar evolution as on Earth is taking place, or has already taken place, on countless other planets in the universe.

Research into evolution has only just begun, and a great deal is still unexplained. Science has not yet addressed, for example, the concept that the evolution of the world – from the state of rest and equilibrium onwards – could not have begun, could not have continued constantly in the same direction and, among other things, could not have given rise to the laws of nature, unless there were in effect a permanent, correspondingly directed *evolution-drive.*

Also the following considerations indicate the presence of an evolution-drive:

(1) The *first* energy form that arose out of unstructured energy could not have developed further without the influence of an evolution-drive, since no other energy form was yet in existence and therefore no mutually-changing influencing was possible.

(2) Once several energy forms came into existence, the chance mutual influencing began. The energy forms now had the possibilities of evolving further, staying the same or disintegrating. The probability that they would stay the same or disintegrate was not only greater than the probability that they would evolve further but was *almost a certainty.* This probability hurdle has been overcome by energy forms – so says science – through constantly repeated trying and "self-organization". For that, however, the time would not have been enough, for example the time on Earth for the evolution up to the present state – which has been calculated by computer. As we know, the evolution proceeded from stage to stage astonishingly fast; the participation of a permanent evolution-drive seems therefore very likely.

(3) If evolution through chance and "self-organization" alone were possible, countless energy forms and natural laws completely foreign to us must have developed elsewhere in space – on and between the cosmic bodies – in part because, by the laws of probability, the chance events necessary for evolution there would have turned out quite different from those on Earth. But, insofar as we have been able to determine, similar energy forms as on Earth and the same natural laws as on Earth have evolved elsewhere in space – in part billions of years before the creation of Earth. This uniform evolution is un-

thinkable without an over-all, uniformly operating evolution-drive.

(4) The emergence everywhere of the natural number which mathematicians call *phi* or the "Golden Mean" is unimaginable without a "drive" that is always operating in the same direction.

(5) Many revelations throughout the ages have illuminated a primary cause of evolution:

    Chinese philosophers already 5,000 years ago mentioned a primary cause (One) – the *Tao* – whereby the *Prime Force* (Zero) was activated and kept going. [Zero and One are the basis of the binary numbering system known in China for thousands of years, ... with which the world with all its forms and happenings can be comprehended mathematically.]
    150 years ago *J. W. Goethe* spoke of "the constantly-active, beneficially-creative force" and in the 20th Century the Nobel prize winner *Ch. S. Sherrington* spoke of "the law that is older than life itself".

This primary cause of evolution, the evolution-drive, can be imagined, for example, as an infinitely fine high-frequency vibration constantly operating in the same direction in all energy particles and therefore also in the cells of our bodies.

After what has been said above – and without evidence to the contrary – it is to be assumed that an evolution-drive is constantly working and that man and his environment are *not* a product *only* of chance and "self-organization".

Regulating structures

The energy forms – man, animals, plants, substances, gases, etc. – are all parts of the universal unity. With their "living", their behavior, they influence each other and themselves.

Through this "influencing", energy forms constantly receive vast numbers of "impressions", bits of information. These are stored by the energy forms insofar as they can. The ability to receive them and the accuracy of the storage grow with the increasing complexity of the energy forms.

The stored information, the imprinted impressions, build the programs and mechanisms which – based on "experiences" from the past – trigger, guide and regulate the development and maintenance of the energy forms in coexistence with each other. We call them the *regulating structures.* [6]

The regulating structures are: the physical and chemical behavior programs – "properties" – of ra-

---

[6] Reasons for the term "regulating structures":
These structures come about through the influencing of energy forms and they regulate the latter's subsequent behavior. The regulation of behavior is the only recognizable purpose of these structures. (Scientific terms for these structures – such as, for example, "matrix" – have not been used since they do not bring out their *essentially* directive aspect.)

diation, atoms, gases and substances; the inherited behavior programs of plants, animals and man; and the information-imprints registered by energy forms during their individual lives as a result of new experiences with the inner and outer world.

The triggering and guidance of the behavior that shapes the lives of the energy forms occur automatically through the regulating structures. Even a man's *consciously* initiated behavior – his conscious thought and action – is automatically brought about by the regulating structures of his mental system.

Research into the regulating structures has only just begun. However, it has already been proven, among other things, that the highly complicated regulating structures of man, containing all of the regulating programs and mechanisms for the construction, maintenance and reproduction of the body, as well as those for behavior – including feeling, thinking and acting – are stored in his cells on spiral molecules of deoxyribonucleic acid (DNA).

What is the purpose of our lives?

The purpose of the changing energy forms

Many gifted people in the course of the last five thousand years have supposed that the world with all its forms consists of a single "Prime Force" – energy. And now this opinion is shared by more and more scientists.

But human intelligence is not yet advanced enough to comprehend the origin and goal of the Prime Force – energy – or the size and duration of the universe. Also still unknown is how the evolution of energy begins; how the highest stages of its organization – its concentrations – are brought about; and whether, when these are achieved, a new evolutionary phase begins with a loosening of the concentrations; and what happens afterwards.

But the boundaries of human knowledge are constantly expanding. And one day even these enigmas will be explained.

Yet what man today knows about energy enables him already to grasp the purpose of structured forms and thereby the purpose of his own life.

Let us consider:

Energy is the building material of the universe. All its known forms are continuously changing. Yet the energy – the Prime Force – is wholly preserved; only its structures and state of motion change. All energy forms – including man – are evolutionary transitions to other forms. The purpose of the changing energy forms, and therefore also the *meaning and purpose of man's existence,* is to be a *transition and step in the course of evolution.*

How do we recognize the rightness and worth of our thoughts and actions?

Pro-evolution – anti-evolution

Cosmic evolution, from the simplest to ever more complex and conscious energy forms, is the cause of our existence; it is the constructive, positive, the *fundamental* "good".

Whatever is directed against cosmic evolution – whatever works against it – is the obstructive, negative, the "bad", "evil".

A person's thoughts and actions that *further* his own evolution and that of his environment are in tune with cosmic evolution, work in the same direction; they are *pro-evolution.*

A person's thoughts and actions that *impair* his own evolution and that of his environment work against – obstruct – cosmic evolution; they are *anti-evolution.*

The correspondence – the harmony – of the behavior of energy forms (man, animals, etc.) with cosmic evolution, we call *pro-evolution-ness.*

Pro-evolution-ness is the objective and unfailing measure for judging the rightness and worth of the behavior of energy forms; it is therefore also the *absolutely certain ethical standard*:

right, good, sensible, valuable is that which promotes evolution – that which is *pro-evolution;*[7]

wrong, bad, evil, senseless is that which impairs evolution – that which is *anti-evolution.*[7]

---

[7] The abbreviations *"pro-evo"* and *"anti-evo"* are used hereafter in this book, in lieu of the more cumbersome "pro-evolution" and "anti-evolution".

How can we consciously create joy and well-being?

Pro-evo thoughts and actions produce joy and well-being; anti-evo thoughts and actions cause unhappiness and harm.

A person's *pro-evo* thoughts and actions further him and his environment. They are in accord with cosmic evolution – the stream of life in and around him. Through this correspondence there arises in him a harmonious "field" that releases in him the feeling of true *joy* – inner lightness and happiness;[8] and his life, in interaction with his environment, unfolds in the best possible way.

The pro-evo thinking and acting person is happy, relaxed and well balanced. His existence is in harmony with the universe.

Anti-evo thoughts and actions of a person damage his own evolution and that of his environment. They are not in correspondence with the evolution-trend of the cosmos. They disturb, obstruct, the stream of life in him and the environment.

---

[8] Compare:

Bertrand Russell, "In a deep, instinctive union with the stream of life lies the greatest of all happiness".

W. Gruter, J. S. Danielli, G. B. Hoebel, "Evidently altruism and 'correct' behavior are rewarded by a release of happiness-inducing endorphins".

Irenäus Eibl-Eibesfeld, "Correct behavior causes, through changes in brain chemistry, hormonal well-being".

The dissonance, conflict, between *anti-evo* thinking or acting and cosmic evolution produces misconduct, morbid conditions, tensions in the person and between him and his environment. *Anti-evo* thoughts and actions cause *unhappiness, discord, harm.*

The anti-evo thinking and acting person is at every step and turn endangered and without true joy.

Anti-evo thoughts and actions also hinder the achievement of genuine, lasting "success". *Whatever is directed against the evolution of energy forms – against life – cannot last. Everything anti-evo disintegrates – sometimes slowly, sometimes fast, sometimes as if struck by lightning.*

Summary

These ideas present a new picture of the cosmos and set forth a new standard for all thinking and acting:

(1) The *world* with all its forms consists of energy. Energy is the *all-embracing, indissoluble organism of the universe.*

(2) The *forms* of energy – man and his environment, concentrations of energy – are as a whole constantly changing in the same fixed direction.

(3) *Pro-evolution-ness* (correspondence – harmony – with cosmic evolution) is the objective and dependable measure for judging the rightness and worth of the behavior of energy forms, of thinking and acting, etc. It is thus the *absolutely certain ethical standard.* Therefore consistent application of the *pro-evolution-ness principle* makes possible the optimizing of human conduct and life.

(4) *Pro-evo* thoughts and actions alone are *right, good, valuable, sensible. They produce joy and well-being. They further life* (the evolution of energy forms) according to the degree of their pro-evolution-ness.

(5) *Anti-evo* thoughts and actions are *wrong, evil, bad, senseless. They produce unhappiness and harm. They damage life* according to the degree of their deviation from *pro-evolution-ness.*

Scientific conceptions about the prime force, the evolution-drive or the regulating structures may differ today or tomorrow from the descriptions in this book.

Such possible differences *in no way detract from the important insight for a person's conduct that only his or her pro-evo (life-promoting, in harmony with evolution) thoughts and actions create true joy and well-being and that his or her anti-evo (life-damaging, evolution-hindering) ideas and deeds unavoidably sooner or later produce unhappiness and harm.*

The following Parts II and III of this book set forth *facets* of the foregoing view of the world and life, and *examples* of the application of the new insights. They are to help the reader to identify reliably what is *pro-evo* and, by behaving accordingly, to *live in joy*.

The following sections deal for the most part with individual topics, and are intended to be read singly and "meditatively" rather than all at once.

Part II

Aspects of the New View of the World and Life

Universal Unity
Evolution-Drive
Regulating Structures
Living in Joy

The energy-organism of the cosmos – the universal unity

The organism of the world

The world with all its forms as it is comprehended by mankind today consists apparently of energy – "Prime Force". Energy constitutes the "organism" in which everything is contained. Nothing and no one is outside it. It is the universal unity.

(For the sake of simplicity, unstructured energy – the unformed – is also termed an energy form in this book.)

Our body – a minute cell of the universe

Our body, with the environment, with all other energy forms – our fellow men, animals, plants, substances, gases, rays, unstructured energy, etc. –, forms the universal unity. Countless bonds unite our body with the other forms. It is inseparably interwoven and connected with them in an infinite, unfathomable system of mutual influences and relationships. In the universal unity, the organism of the universe, it is a minute, constantly changing "cell".

Our body – conscious energy

The world consists of energy. Our body – part of the energy of the world – recognizes this fact through its capacity for reflective thought. In this way the *energy in our body has become conscious of itself.* It now sees itself in our body and in all other forms as the universal unity – the all-embracing One and Only.

The universal unity – our true self

We recognize ourselves as part of the universal unity – and the universal unity as our true self. Nothing is "foreign" to us any longer. We ourselves are everything. We are freed from the confines of our human bodies and feel that we are boundless. When we look at the universe, we are looking at ourselves …

No distinction between You and Me

All human beings are part of the all-embracing energy unity. Through this recognition, the barriers between You and Me fade away.

The effect of our behavior within the universal unity

Our body, our fellow human beings and all the other energy forms of our environment together constitute the organism of the universal unity.

Anything we do that is beneficial or harmful to our body is therefore also beneficial or harmful to our fellow human beings and the rest of the environment; similarly, if we benefit or harm others or the environment we also benefit or harm ourselves.

We are inseparably joined with everything else in

the universal unity – the infinitely interwoven "network" that is the universe.

The energy of the universe remains constant

The "amount" of energy remains constant. Nothing is lost, nothing is added. When energy particles apparently vanish, this only means that they have assumed forms that are not yet recognizable by man.

Evolution-drive

The cause of creation

The considerations under "Are we a product of chance?" in Part I above indicate that a life drive (evolution-drive) is active, that sets evolution in motion – the "creation" – and that causes it to continue from stage to stage.[9]

According to this assumption, the life-drive is also the primary cause of quantum leaps and mutations; and when, as a result of the formation of regulating structures that inhibit evolution (e. g., through "aging") or as a result of destructive environmental influences, energy forms decline into simpler forms, they are reinvolved through the life-drive in the evo-

---

[9] It is perhaps an infinitely fine, high frequency vibration – the elemental sound of life (compare AUM or OM) – caused by a phenomenon like cosmic background radiation, that constantly flows through all energy-particles.

lution of more intensive and complex energy concentrations, so that in the universe evolution as a whole continues in the same forward direction.

The cosmic order principle

Whatever area of existence we investigate, we always encounter – evidently as a result of the unceasing, evenly directed influence of the life-drive on all energy particles – "order" (physical, chemical, mathematical and acoustical/musical laws, interval proportions, systems, analogies, etc.), whose origin was in the past attributed to, among other things, the "world soul"[10] or to divine or known physical and chemical influences.[11]

---

[10] Plato: Timaeus.

[11] Compare also: Weltharmonik (*J. Kepler*); Lehrbuch der Harmonik (textbook of harmonics) (*H. Kayser*); Der messbare Einklang (measurable harmony) (*R. Haase*); etc. Examples of research results in this area: the arrangement of the human body according to harmonic interval proportions (*G. Hildebrandt*); harmonic laws in the arrangement of full-grown crystals (*V. Goldschmidt*); the ordering of the elements according to their nuclear charges (ordinal numbers, numbers of electrons): this series of natural numbers is identical with the law governing the progression of the harmonic series – in other words there is an analogy with the most important harmonic natural law (*R. Haase*); the harmonic interval proportions in the completed planet system (*J. Kepler*).

Harmony

Sounds, forms, colors and behavior which we find harmonious are probably perfectly tuned to the life-drive, in unison with its “wavelength”.

Space and duration

Space and duration in the infinite universe can be measured only in those areas where evolution is taking place, relative to its phenomena: duration is measured in terms of “time”, and spatial expanse in terms of “height”, “width” and “depth”.

Regulating structures

Mutual influence

Our behavior – our “manifestations of life” – and that of our fellow human beings and the other energy forms around us influence both us and them. This “information” creates impressions – regulating structures – in us and in them, insofar as the ability to receive and store such impressions has been developed. Since the beginning of evolution, the behavior of individual energy forms has influenced both themselves and, more or less strongly, all other energy forms. *All events in the universe influence everything – since the very beginning.*

The more alike the regulating structures of the energy forms are to one another, the more comprehensive and exact their reception and storage of mutual influences will be. Energy forms with similar regulating structures are well-tuned transmitters and receivers of each other's manifestations of life.

Regulating structures operate either *pro-evo* or *anti-evo* according to the internal and external "experiences" which formed them.

Man's regulating structures

Man's regulating structures have been formed in the course of the evolution of atoms, gases, solids, plants, animals and his human ancestors – and during his own life through his "experiences" with the environment. They direct his life; they regulate the physical and chemical activities of his body cells and all his behavior including his emotions, thoughts and actions. [12]

---

[12] The past is more or less clearly recorded in man's regulating structures. His knowledge, perceptions and conceptions are combinations and copies of this stored "experience". Even his prophetic (precognitive) capabilities, such as the foretelling of coming events in dreams and other "acausal" happenings, are expressions of the regulating structures. Appropriately sensitive people such as clairvoyants or people in situations of extreme emergency can even read stored "impressions" from individual events and precisely reconstruct them.
(The action potential contained in man's regulating structures is largely realized without his conscious assistance.)

Man's heritage

Man's "heritage" is not limited to the regulating structures of his cells. Other aspects of his heritage include experience and knowledge preserved in pictures, writings and sound.

But it is man's regulating structures, his thought mechanisms, that, have enabled the preservation of knowledge and experience in these forms as well as the production of all other "artificial" things.

Realization, actualization, of thoughts

Thoughts – their vibrations – imprint regulating structures which automatically actualize, or seek to actualize, the thoughts.

Therefore negativism, complaining, contempt, self-pity, reproach, or fears about a possible illness or other misfortune, should absolutely be avoided, and even unimportant thoughts should be *pro-evo, – life-promoting, positive, affirmative, unshakably confident.*

The more often the same thoughts are repeated and the more vivid they are, the stronger and more pronounced will be the corresponding regulating structures, which then help set the course of our behavior.

If there is *doubt* about the possible actualization of a thought, idea or desired goal, effective regulating structures will not be imprinted.

The actualization of thoughts is still scientifically largely unresearched.

Perhaps the regulating structures created by thoughts act on unstructured or weakly structured energy – which appears to be present everywhere in and between atoms – and cause it to structure itself and function in particular ways.[13]

(1) *Healing through thought:*

There are countless reports of the healing of minor, serious and "incurable" illnesses through thought (imagining a cure, autosuggestion or heterosuggestion, etc.). Not much is known about the technique of healing through thought, and unfortunately little research was done into the methods of famous healers by suggestion, such as the French pharmacologist Coué.

Self-healing through conscious thought probably works in the following way: in his thoughts – triggered by reports of cures, his own experiences of healing, autosuggestion, religious ideas, etc. – the patient forms a clear, vivid image of certain recovery, which firmly "imprints", or "forms", the corresponding regulating structures. And these in turn automatically effect a cure; they make the idea, the mental picture, *real.*

---

[13] This hypothesis would, for example, explain the unimpeded effect of long-distance hypnotic commands sent to a person in a lead cage 1700 km away (see Professor *L. L. Vassiliev*'s experiments) and other examples of the influence of thought on people, animals, plants, material substances or objects.

In *hypnosis*, while the patient is asleep or in a trance, the regulating structures that will trigger the healing process are directly imprinted through the mental influence of the hypnotist – leaving out the detour through the patient's conscious thought processes.

Healing effected by *placebos* is also a form of cure by thought. (Placebos are imitation drugs which look and taste just like them – but do not contain their healing substances.) Patients given placebos – without being told what they really are – *believe* they are taking the real thing. They expect the beneficial effect attributed to the medication. In, their minds they produce the idea, the mental image of this cure, thus forming the corresponding regulating structures – which then in most subjects of placebo experiments actually bring about the expected cure.

(2) *Muscle relaxation, feeling warm and cold, etc.:*

If we imagine – think – that the muscles of our arms and legs are relaxed, then corresponding regulating structures will be formed which will automatically bring about the relaxation of the muscles. Feelings of warmth and cold and other sensations and "achievements" can also be brought about by appropriate thoughts.[14]

[14] Compare, among other works, "Das autogene Training" (Autogenic Training) by *J. H. Schultz* (A. Thieme Verlag).

(3) *Hunting ritual:*

Before a hunt, the pygmies draw an antelope in the sand, and with the first ray of sunlight shoot an arrow at it. They then go hunting and come home with an antelope that has been hit by an arrow in the same place as in the drawing.

The ritual – the drawing and symbolic slaying of the antelope – is conducted in absolute silence. In this silence and concentration on the idea – the image – regulating structures are imprinted which "trigger" the actual shooting of the antelope.

Examples of inadequate regulating structures

(1) The turkey hen recognizes its chick only by its chirping. If it does not chirp, she kills it, on the "instinctive assumption" that the chick is either an enemy or is too weak to survive. Yet she will mother a dummy polecat, her deadly enemy, with a built-in recording of the appropriate chirping sound.

(2) When human regulating structures for self-preservation are pathologically overaccentuated, they can trigger a striving for "power" or the accumulation of possessions that are not necessary for a *pro-evo* existence, or other exaggerated personal or political protective measures.

What causes differences

What makes energy forms different from one another are the regulating structures – the "imprints" of their different pasts – and the forms and modes of behavior caused by the regulating structures and by the environment.

The disintegration of regulating structures

When energy forms decay, they break down into forms with simpler regulating structures; and probably also into unstructured energy if the regulating structures disintegrate completely as, for example, under the influence of heat.[15]

The past and future potential of man

In man his past – his "experiences" since the beginning of evolution – is stored fairly plainly and accurately in his regulating structures.

---

[15] In light of the principles of thermodynamics, structured energy, which can be reincorporated into new forms through the evolution drive, is more conceivable and satisfactory as the final result of an evolutionary cycle than the hypothesis of total and final extinction. Furthermore, no evolution cycle will end with the decomposition of all structures once energy forms – such as man – reach a level of consciousness that enables them to determine the future course of evolution in a *pro-evo* way, towards goals unimaginable today (unless this is prevented by environmental conditions).

His future evolution will be the product of the interaction of his regulating structures with the evolution-drive and the environment.

Man's past and his future potential are thus present within him.[16]

Rapid progress by consciously influencing the regulating structures

In the future, man will increasingly be able to influence *consciously* both his own regulating structures and those of other energy forms in a *pro-evo* way.[17]

As a result, the evolution of energy within man's sphere of efficacy will proceed with hitherto unimagined speed.

---

[16] Thus the prophetic (precognitive) ability of man can be seen as a synthesis within the unconscious.

[17] Through, for example, *appropriate* consciously generated mental images, education and training, specially prepared foods and genetic intervention.

Pro-evo guideline – the ethic of joy

Traditional ethical concepts and rules arose from mankind's experiences and from the interpretation and application of these experiences to future behavior.

In the past, determination of fundamental ethical principles depended on man's intellectual capacity and knowledge at the time, on his living conditions, on religious ideas, and on arbitrary decisions motivated by non-ethical concerns.

Behavior which was thought *right, good, valuable* or *sensible* was that which promoted or seemed to promote the ways of life, social systems and goals that people, or their lawmakers, considered desirable at the time; behavior which was thought *wrong, evil, bad* or *senseless* was that which impaired or seemed to impair them.

Today we know that there is an *objective guideline for judging the rightness and value of thoughts and actions: pro-evolution-ness* (the accordance – the harmony – of behavior with cosmic evolution, the stream of life). Ethical standards are now exactly determinable and definable with the help of the new guideline:

> *right, good, valuable and sensible* are those thoughts and actions which promote life, the evolution of energy forms – man and his environment – and which therefore are *pro-life (pro-*

> *evo); wrong, evil, bad* and *senseless* is behavior which *does not promote, or which harms, the life of energy forms: the anti-life (anti-evo).*

If a person thinks and acts in a *pro-evo* way, if his behavior is life-promoting – operating in the same direction as cosmic evolution, the stream of life – a harmonic "field" arises in him, producing a feeling of *joy;* and he relates to other people and the rest of the environment in the best possible way.

If a person thinks and acts in an *anti-evo* way – if his thoughts and actions obstruct and damage the stream of life, his own development and that of his environment – distorted attitudes, unhealthy conditions and tension arise within him and between him and his environment; his life is then endangered at every turn and without true *joy.*

Since the rightness and value of behavior, thoughts and actions are dependent on their effect on cosmic evolution – the *evolution of the universal unity, of the energy forms as a whole* – the following should be noted:

> Behavior that would be *pro-evo* for one or more energy forms is *anti-evo* if the *universal unity* – to which these energy forms and all others belong – *is harmed more than benefited by it. Example:* Improving the living conditions of an individual, race or nation – as such, a *pro-evo* measure – is *anti-evo* if other people are thereby harmed in an intolerable way and *more disadvantage than advantage, or avoidable harm, results* for mankind as a whole, and hence for the *universal unity.*

Behavior which would be *anti-evo* for one or more energy forms is *pro-evo* if the *universal unity is benefited to a greater extent than it is harmed.* Example: Killing someone – as such, an *anti-evo* action – is nevertheless *pro-evo* if the individual is threatening the lives of his fellow men and they can be saved only if he is killed.

Helpful questions for evaluating the degree to which our thoughts and actions are pro-evo – generating joy and well-being

(1) Do our thoughts and actions *further* our own development (that of our body, intellectual capacity and living conditions) in the best possible way, without thereby intolerably harming other people and/or the rest of our surroundings?

(2) Do our thoughts and actions *further* the development of other people and the rest of our surroundings in the best possible way without thereby endangering or harming our own development?

Joy through conscious and unconscious life-promoting thought and action

A person's life will evolve in the best possible way and in *joy* if he consciously or unconsciously – for example, by chance or as a consequence of a particular philosophical or religious outlook – thinks and acts in a *pro-evo* way.

If someone unconsciously behaves in a way that is entirely *pro-evo*, one speaks of grace. Scarcely one life in a million is lived in grace.

But through conscious *pro-evo* thought and action every one of us can live in *joy.*

Joy does not depend on material goods and natural gifts

True *joy* can be achieved only by *pro-evo* thoughts and deeds – not by material goods or gifts, wealth, power, youth or marked intellectual ability.

Joy is not dependent on any particular type of activity

All activities, whether training for a career, cleaning the street, governing a state, caring for the sick or ploughing a field, fill people with *joy* when they carry them out to the best of their abilities in a *pro-evo* way – a way that harmonizes as nearly as possible with the stream of life in them and in the environment.

Joy does not depend on the kind of activity, but on the degree to which the activity is carried out in a *pro-evo* way.

Joy is independent of utility

A scientist with his more highly developed intellectual capability and specialized knowledge can contribute incomparably more to society as a whole than can, for example, a bricklayer with his *pro-evo* work on a building. But both, through their *pro-evo* behavior – their effort to carry out their work in the best possible way – win *joy,* inner happiness, in about equal measure.

Everyone can live in joy – it is entirely up to us

No two people are alike; everyone is unique. The circumstances that surround us also differ. However, everyone can live in *joy* through *pro-evo* thought and action – regardless of talents and circumstances. It is entirely up to us.

Even a blind person, with amputated hands and feet, can find *joy* through consciousness of the eternal energy unity and *pro-evo* thought and action – for example, by bearing his pain and wants in a conscious, exemplary way that inspires and helps other people come to terms with their own difficulties, or by comforting or teaching others.

Inexhaustible opportunities for joy

Every human being, in every situation, has inexhaustible opportunities to think and act in a *pro-evo* way – and hence has inexhaustible opportunities to live in *joy.*

Joy – the yardstick for human behavior

True *joy* is the sure sign that a person is behaving in a *pro-evo*, life-promoting way. If he is joyless, gloomy, sullen, bad-tempered, dissatisfied, restless, insecure, anxiety-ridden or cynical, – then his thoughts and actions are still in some way *anti-evo.*

Traditional ethical rules can serve as guidelines for pro-evo behavior

Many traditional ethical concepts and rules, such as "Do good and avoid evil", "Love thy neighbor", "Tell the truth", "Thou shall not steal", "Thou shall not kill", "Honor thy father and thy mother", "Behave decently", "Be chivalrous", etc., are for the most part *pro-evo*, and to a large extent we can use them to guide our behavior.

We must, however, be careful: these traditional ethical concepts and principles arose out of human experience and interpretations of experience that were often erroneous or arbitrary. *They are useful guidelines when they encourage behavior that promotes life (evolution); when, however, they encourage behavior that harms life (evolution), they become inappropriate.*

The following are examples of ways in which traditional ethical rules should be revised:

(1) *The commandment to love one's neighbor.*

Loving one's neighbor in the traditional sense requires that we should love our neighbor as ourselves – and if he strikes us, allow him to do so without resistance. This kind of love is to a certain extent *anti-evo.*

The requirement that we should love our neighbor as ourselves is insufficient. We must consciously further our neighbor and love him in a *pro-evo* way. How we treat our own body cannot be used as a guide for loving others. We may love ourselves to an exaggerated extent or we may neglect ourselves; both would be *anti-evo.*[18]

If our neighbor strikes us, he is behaving in an *anti-evo* way – he is harming the universal unity to which we belong and to which he belongs as well. We must therefore properly protect ourselves from him.

(2) *The commandment to love, honor and obey one's parents.*

It is *pro-evo* to love – to further – our parents, regardless of how they behave. Our parents are, like all our fellow human beings, part of the universal energy unity.

However, it is wrong to honor them and praise their behavior if they act in *anti-evo* ways, or to obey them if they demand such behavior of us. We must instead point out their *anti-evo* behavior to them, state clearly that we reject it and also refuse to comply with their *anti-evo* requests or demands.

---

[18] See "*Pro-evo love for others*" and "*Helping without harming*" below in this "Living in joy" Section.

(3) *The commandment to tell the truth.*

Untruths in any form, blatant and concealed lies, creating false impressions, etc., are *anti-evo.* They produce disorder, conflict and harm. They destroy trust between people. Even small or thoughtless lies often have a very bad effect on the liars.

However, so-called white lies can be *pro-evo*, when, for example, they are the only way of protecting people's lives. In such a case a deliberate lie is necessary to prevent a greater evil – something more *anti-evo* than the white lie.

(4) *The commandment not to steal.*

People who steal from others are acting in an *anti-evo* way. They are harming both those they steal from and the human community as a whole; the latter because they are breaking the prohibition against stealing that protects the community from chaotic property ownership and its consequences.

There are, however, exceptions. Theft can be *pro-evo* when, for example, stealing food is the only way to avoid starving.

In order not to weaken the existing prohibition against stealing with such exceptions, the stolen goods should be replaced by the people who have been saved by them; if they are unable to do so, the community as a whole should make good the loss.

(5) *The commandment not to kill.*

Man is the most highly developed of all known forms of energy and is therefore the most worthy of protection. As long as a person lives, there is normally a possibility that he will consciously think and act in a *pro-evo* way – thereby promoting the evolution of the universal unity. Human life should thus end only at its absolute biological limit.

Killing someone – prematurely ending his life by, for example, shooting him or inflicting avoidable harm on him over a long period of time – is therefore particularly *anti-evo.*

However, killing a murderer in self-defense is *pro-evo* if this is the only way of preventing other deaths. Similarly, killing someone who will never be capable of thinking and acting *consciously* – because, for example, of irreversible brain damage – can also be *pro-evo* – if the doctors, the relatives and the general public are convinced that this would entail a release both for the unconscious person and other people. In the case of such agreement, the general prohibition against killing – which protects life in society – will be neither obscured nor relaxed.

Exact research into pro-evo behavior

The *pro-evo principle* makes possible scientific research and determinations regarding optimal behavior.

With increasing knowledge and the help of computers, man will be able to identify *pro-evo* goals and behavior with ever-increasing accuracy.

And the more mankind's goals and behavior – with respect to nutrition, clothing, housing, health care, education, training, service to the community and human relationships, etc. – promote life, the more they are *pro-evo*, then the more harmonious will be our existence, and the more we will experience joy and well-being.

Everything else will become unimportant and bearable

As soon as a person has identified his *pro-evo* goals and modes of behavior – those which produce joy and well-being – and persists in actualizing them, everything else becomes immaterial; his physical shortcomings become bearable, feelings of inferiority and other psychological problems disappear, etc.

Avoid what is anti-evo at all costs

A person's *anti-evo* goals and behavior disturb the stream of life in him and in his environment, and thereby produce unhappiness, discord, restlessness and harm. All things that are not necessary for a *pro-evo* existence also burden and hinder.

Avoid and omit everything that does not promote life or that harms it, everything *anti-evo*. Even a single word which serves no *pro-evo* purpose is too much.

Only thought and action focused on promoting life – evolution – in ourselves and our environment brings joy and happiness.

Pro-evo goals prevent anti-evo behavior

Both our *pro-evo* and *anti-evo* thoughts and actions produce regulating structures which correspondingly influence our conscious and unconscious behavior.

Anti-evo behavior should therefore not be directly "fought"; its causes, the regulating structures which trigger it, would only be reinforced by a more intensive preoccupation with them.

Anti-evo behavior – impoliteness, resentment, envy, jealousy, quarrelling, hostility, slander, untruthfulness, deceit, robbery, avarice, brutality, hate, torturing and killing people and animals, contempt, cowardice, laziness, indifference, immoderation, disorder, dirtiness, anger, self-pity, arrogance, despair, lust, inaccuracy, anxiety, fanaticism, rage and so on – *disappear of their own accord, or do not arise at all, if a person sets only pro-evo goals and persistently seeks to achieve them.*

Wasted effort

When we think and act in *anti-evo* ways, we exhaust ourselves in vain. We also achieve no lasting "success" and sooner or later destroy more than we may temporarily achieve.

Wrong behavior

If *anti-evo* behavior is abandoned as soon as it is recognized, *pro-evo* goals can nevertheless still be attained and any harm done in the meantime can be overcome.

There is a *pro-evo* way out of even the most tangled situation. The *pro-evo principle* is an infallible compass.

Best living conditions

In all thought and action, we should preserve and protect our *own* existence – our potential and vitality.

We should further our body (both its physical and mental aspects) in every way and create the best circumstances for ourselves – without harming others.

Concentrated, joyful endeavors in pursuit of our *pro*-life goals, and sufficient, enjoyable recreation – challenging and relaxing – should alternate harmoniously.

The "good things in life" should also be enjoyed, provided they benefit our health, invigorate us and do no one any harm – otherwise they should be avoided.

Pro-evo love for others

The aware person understands himself and his fellow men as concentrations of energy, as large molecules of the infinite energy organism of the universe. He knows that he is inseparably connected with his fellow men and all other energy forms in this universal unity – he feels himself as "one" with them.

It is hence impossible for him to reject or even be indifferent to others. He furthers them, their circumstances, their intellectual capacity and their awareness as much as he can without endangering the *pro-evo* course of his own existence.

The best possible way of furthering others – without at the same time jeopardizing one's own *pro-evo* development and *pro-evo* existence – is *pro-evo love of others.*

Reject the anti-evo behavior of other people – never the people themselves

We should *firmly reject* the *anti-evo* goals and behavior of other people and of human organizations (countries, regions, communities, businesses, unions, etc.), *warn against them and indicate the pro-evo goals and behavior that should be pursued.*

But the form of the rejection and warning should show clearly that *we love the others without qualification – that we desire to further them – and reject only their anti-evo goals and behavior.* We should therefore never reproach people for their mistakes, condemn, insult or hurt them.

Helping without harming

We should help others through words and actions insofar as this does not endanger the *pro-evo* course of our own existence.

However, we should never take on or remove their problems and duties if they could master them themselves with sufficient effort. This would be inviting them to take advantage of us whether consciously or unconsciously – and would be taking away from them the opportunity to learn how to overcome difficulties by themselves; *we would be irresponsibly weakening them, and reducing their ability to cope with life.*

Confusion will not arise

We should ask ourselves before all decisions, words and actions whether they are *pro-evo* – whether they promote the life, the evolution, of ourselves and our environment. If our behavior is *pro-evo,* our life will unfold in the best possible way.

Calm and persistent

We should pursue our small and large *pro-evo* goals with persistence – calmly, simply, matter-of-factly, and as much as possible unnoticed by others, so that they do not distract us.

Our plans should not, however, fail because of our own rigidity. We must temporarily adapt ourselves to insurmountable circumstances and flexibly circumvent obstacles.

"Water cannot overturn boulders; it flows around them, hollows them out – and unfailingly reaches its goal, the sea."[19]

Fountain of youth

Our life-promoting thoughts and actions, the *pro-evo* goals, that we seek to actualize, hold us in tension, stimulate our cells to renew themselves and keep us young right up to the furthest biologically possible limit of life.

Laziness, cowardice

If we are too lazy or too cowardly to discover and pursue our *pro-evo* goals and duties, then we should not be surprised at the circumstances under which we have to live or into which we are led.

A daily reminder

In order never to forget to think and act in a *pro-evo* way – bringing about joy and well-being –, we should resolve afresh every morning:

to carry out our pro-evo tasks for the day as thoroughly and quickly as possible;

---

[19] Lao Tzu.

to further others, and never harm them;

to be steadfastly truthful.

If every day we seek with firm resolve to carry out these important guidelines, we will soon feel their beneficial effects and *pro-evo* thought and action in all circumstances will become a habit.

Self-examination

When we are without joy, unhappy or morose, in a bad mood, irritable, restless or discontented, then our behavior has in some way not been *pro-evo.* We should immediately re-evaluate our goals, tasks and modes of behavior: give up the *anti-evo* ones we find and replace them with *pro-evo* ones, so that we can be filled with *joy* and our life unfold in the best possible way.[20]

The importance of our thoughts and actions for the evolution of the universe and for ourselves

For the evolution of the infinitely large energy-organism of the cosmos, it is immaterial whether our thoughts and actions are *pro-evo* or *anti-evo.* The evolution-drive will always again effortlessly bring the effects of our erroneous behavior back into its own direction.

Our *anti-evo* behavior is far less of a hindrance to

---

[20] See "Some questions for weekly examination of one's own behavior" in Part III below.

the evolution of the energy unity than a grain of sand to a rushing mountain torrent.

For example, even if we were to destroy all mankind with atomic bombs, yet in a few tens of millions of years beings with minds and consciousness will probably have developed on our planet again. This event that seems so monstrous to us would in no way hold up evolution on Earth and would be insignificant in terms of the universe.

However, for the sake of our own lives and the lives of those around us, it is crucial that we think and act in a pro-evo way. Only those thoughts and actions that promote life – that harmonize with evolution, the stream of life – bring *joy,* benefit, inner peace and well-being. Our *anti-evo* thoughts and actions sooner or later inevitably produce unhappiness and harm.

The commandment

Steadfastly think and act pro-evo: establish pro-evo goals, tasks and modes of behavior for all areas and in every situation of life – and energetically realize them.

Nothing else need concern us.

Thinking and acting *pro-evo* gives rise in us to true *joy* – the feeling of inner lightness and happiness – and our lives will unfold in the best possible way.

Thinking and acting *anti-evo,* we are endangered at every step and turn and are without true *joy.*

Optimal life

Several times a day we should test whether our thoughts and actions are *pro-evo*. If they are not, we should correct them right away. And harmony and joy will fill us again.

Part III

Examples of Applying the New Insights

Including Clarification of Questions and Enigmas that Have Long Occupied Mankind

From the paradise of unconsciousness to the paradise of consciousness – the "Age of Joy"

The "mirroring" of thoughts – reflective thinking – produces consciousness.

Around three million years ago the unconscious animal predecessor of man changed – through the arising of reflective thinking in him – into a conscious animal, man.

In that remote age he began to use stone axes and fire systematically. This marked the end of the paradise of unconscious life, in which man's predecessor lived without conscious thought or action, "without cares, anxiety or responsibility". ("He ate from the tree of knowledge and thereby lost paradise.")

The period which followed, when man's capacity for reflective thought gradually developed and activities which had previously been unconscious increasingly became conscious – such as planning for the future, satisfying sexual desires and other basic instincts, etc. – was a period of uncertainty, of laborious searching for the right ways of behavior.

The development of reflective thinking has led over a rough road, over countless errors and mistakes, to our present stage of consciousness. Perhaps the greatest and gravest of man's past errors was his supposition that he was independent from his environment and possessed an "independent self".

The period of great uncertainty, of slowly dawning consciousness, is now coming to an end. Man is recognizing that he is part of the energy unity of the universe – and in him, through this knowledge, energy has become conscious of itself.

About three million years ago, when reflective thinking began to develop, the *paradise of unconsciousness* was lost. And at the present time, there opens for man, through his more developed capacity for thought, a new phase in his evolution: the *paradise of consciousness*, the "Age of Joy", in which man, as conscious part of the energy unity of the universe, *consciously thinking and acting pro-evo, will live in joy.*

The development of the human faculty for thought in recent millennia

Man's intellectual capacity has hardly changed for tens of thousands of years. The authors of the I Ching, the Vedas or the Egyptian Hermes or Lao Tzu, Confucius, Buddha, Socrates or Plato, for instance, would have been able to understand our most advanced knowledge – more quickly than the average person today.

But knowledge and aids to thinking have increased massively since then. And in the future these will make possible hitherto inconceivable feats of thinking.

Human thinking mostly still unconscious

Some animals show signs of a beginning of reflective thinking. Monkeys use small sticks to get insects out of holes; chimpanzees solve difficult problems involving counting and combination, and use clubs to defend themselves; and modes of behavior exhibited by other animals such as dolphins, dogs and birds also indicate that they are moving towards "deliberate" reflective thinking.

But even animals with highly developed brains, such as dolphins, are probably not aware that they are thinking.

Even with man the greater part of thinking is still unconscious or barely conscious – without conscious direction or awareness of the thought process.

Only a fraction of what is going on in the universe is discernible

Man's reflective thinking can perceive and explain only a small part of the endless profusion of structures, forms and relationships in the universe – and often can hardly determine whether something is "real" or is created by the mind.

Growth of power through increasing consciousness

With the increase in consciousness, man's power – his creative force, his ability to concentrate energy and to dissolve its concentrations – also grows.

Only people with insufficient consciousness behave in anti-evo ways

People who think and act in *anti-evo* ways are inadequately conscious – the result either of deficient intellectual capacity or of never having been enlightened about the energy unity and its evolution.

The absence of the will to behave in *pro-evo* ways is also a consequence of inadequate consciousness.

Conscious control of basic instincts

The more conscious a person becomes, the better he is able to control, change or sublimate his basic instincts (aggression, sexuality, the urge to dominate and possess, etc.) so that they operate only in a *pro-evo* – life promoting and not life harming – way.

(*Man's behavior is determined by his basic instincts only insofar as he – like an animal without consciousness – gives them free rein.*)

Why is conscious man "forced" to think and act in a pro-evo way?

All occurrences in the energy unity are inevitable events of evolution.

Even human endeavor to think and act in *pro-evo* ways is not the result of "free will". It is the inevitable result of reflective thinking.

As soon as a person realizes clearly enough that only *pro-evo* behavior produces *joy* and well-being, while *anti-evo* behavior produces unhappiness and harm, he will persistently strive to think and act only in a *pro-evo* way, and will avoid *anti-evo* thoughts and deeds as a burnt child avoids fire: his reflective thinking causes, or forces, him to do this.

Possibilities for the expansion of consciousness

Man's reflective, conscious thinking has endless possibilities for expansion. Almost all the brain's frontal lobe – which is still largely unused – is available for the expansion of the "consciousness functions" of thinking.

Omniscience

The energy unity of the universe contains all "knowledge" of itself. The individual energy forms become aware of this "knowledge" to the extent that they have developed the necessary organs for consciousness – the awakening of knowledge.

"All knowledge is recollection."[21]

Consciousness, superconsciousness, subconsciousness, deepconsciousness

What man is *conscious* of is what he grasps with his reflective thinking; he is *unconscious* of everything else – the various shifts in evolution over time, the "history".

---

[21] Plato.

Terms such as consciousness, superconsciousness, subconsciousness and deepconsciousness, used up to now, are misleading, inexact, and should be avoided.

Aspects of consciousness

The terms *reason, intellect and mind* refer to unclearly defined, partial aspects and effects of reflective thinking.

Man's most precious faculty

Man's most precious faculty is his capacity for conscious, *pro-evo* thought and action – the conscious promotion of life, of the evolution of the energy forms.

Raising human consciousness is therefore the most important task of education and schools and the prime purpose of one's own pursuit of further knowledge – and *impairing consciousness* with alcohol, drugs, misinformation, etc., is the greatest wrong.

The energy which has become conscious in man consciously influences further evolution

In conscious man, energy has become conscious of itself. It now guides its own evolution within his sphere of influence, conscious through him. Through him it limits the mutual, *accidental* influence – which can be *pro-evo* or *anti-evo* – of its forms on one another and through him it consciously brings the behavior of its forms into increasing harmony with the stream of life.

Within his sphere of influence, conscious man replaces what was previously an unconscious change of energy with more *pro-evo* change. As far as his intellectual capacity and his knowledge permit him, he furthers himself, his fellow men, animals, plants and the rest of the environment in the *way that is best for the evolution of the universal unity* and prevents all avoidable harm.

What is the next recognizable goal of the evolution of the universe?

Evolution proceeds from the *simplest to increasingly complex and more conscious* energy forms.

The *full* consciousness of the energy-organism of the universe appears to be the next goal.

Are we immortal?

Man is a form – a large molecule – in the indivisible unity of energy that is the universe.

Man develops out of the fertilized egg. This seed is invisible to the naked eye. In spite of its minute size it contains all of man's regulating structures that have been formed in the course of the evolution of energy from electromagnetic fields, gases, material substances, plants and animals up to the particular individual's parents.

Man's inherited regulating structures, which are expanded through the "impressions" – the experiences – during his lifetime, direct the development and maintenance of his body and his behavior both in and outside of the womb. From the development of the fertilized egg until the person's death he is constantly absorbing and giving out energy particles – a process brought about by the regulating structures and environmental influences. These energy particles make up the human "form"; they enter man as nutrition, inhaled air and "vibrations" of warmth, feelings, thoughts and so on; they leave him as exhaled air, digestive substances, "vibrations" of warmth, feelings, thoughts, etc., body movements, reproductive seed, and finally as substances, gases, etc., upon the decomposition of his body after death.

No energy particle is lost in the formation, maintenance and decomposition of a human being; but no additional particles are created either.

All energy particles come from the environment, and all return – changed – to it.

Man, like all other forms, is composed of energy – is a concentration of energy. He is a transitory vessel, a fleeting agglomeration of particles within the indivisible energy unity of the universe.

Man's life, measured against the time-span of cosmic evolution, is much shorter than the "blinking of an eye". But his substance, the energy of the particles of which he is constituted – through which he comes into being, lives and dies –, is everlasting. The energy particles which leave the human form are always again reincorporated into new forms.

Man, his form, his body with all its capabilities, is transitory. But his "being" – the content, the energy, which brought about his birth, life and death – is everlasting.

The energy through which man is born, lives and dies – which passes through him – will in the course of evolution constantly be incorporated into new forms and in them will sooner or later become more conscious of itself than is possible in man in his present form with his still incomplete intellectual capacity.

Do we have an "independent" mind?

The course of a person's life is shaped by his regulating structures acting in conjunction with the evolution-drive and environmental influences. His growth and maintenance, his behavior – his thoughts and actions – all stem from these three causes. Even his consciousness develops automatically, as soon as the regulating structures of his mental system contain the functional prerequisites.

Man is a part of the energy unity of the universe, and a product of its evolution. He has no "own" being separate from the energy unity, he is not a being by himself.

How a person's life proceeds, how far it develops in a *pro-evo* or *anti-evo*, conscious or unconscious, way, depends only on the automatically operating formative causes – the person's own regulating structures and environmental influences.

Even man's most conscious thoughts and actions and apparently completely uninfluenced free will are the outcome of these formative causes working together. If, for example, a person consciously sets himself a goal and tries with strong will to achieve it, applying his own creative ideas and inventions, the whole process takes places automatically. It all happens – he does it – because the regulating structure of his mental system, in conjunction with the environmental influences, bring it about.[22]

Man is not an independent being with his "own"

---

[22] From these ideas it also follows that:

(1) the person who is aware of these relationships (whose mind and thoughts are appropriately developed and oriented) will *automatically* strive to think and act only in a *pro-evo* way – in other words to further his own life and that of his environment *with initiative* and *in the best possible way* in every situation, and

(2) this structured *compulsion* to think and act in a *pro-evo* way, producing joy and well-being, could be im-

strength and his "own" thoughts and actions. Whatever he may think or do consciously or unconsciously: all is behavior that occurs automatically within the energy-organism of the universe – through the operation of the causes referred to above.

The limits of knowledge

Everything consists of energy. The energy unity contains everything – even all knowledge about itself.

Man is a part of the energy unity, a concentrated form of energy. For this reason he has access to knowledge about himself and the energy forms of his environment.

This knowledge manifests itself in man, he becomes aware of it, insofar as his intellectual capacity permits.

Today much more is understood by man than was a million, ten thousand, a hundred or even ten years ago. In spite of this progress he can at present only partially and imperfectly understand the universe, the events and relationships in the micro- and macrocosmos. His intellectual capacity is still limited, as is the capacity of his other sense organs. (His eyes, for example, can see of the infinitely many light phe-

---

planted in all people by educating them about those facts – in schools and by means of literature, television, radio, films, etc.

nomena only that fraction with wavelengths between 380 and 760 millionths of a millimeter, and his ears can pick up only sounds with frequencies of between 16 and about 20,000 cycles per second.)

But man's powers of perception are constantly expanding. He is continually producing new aids to further this development, such as machines for calculating and for other thinking processes. He will also improve the capacity of his brain with new thinking methods and by physical and chemical means.[23]

Man will continuously expand his understanding of everything that is still incomprehensible today.

And the more he knows, the more conscious he becomes, then the more he will live in a *pro-evo* way and therefore in greater joy and happiness.

The limits of power

Man is a conscious part of the energy-unity of the universe. Therefore, he has within himself the power to assemble and divide energy – to concentrate it and dissolve its concentrations.

This creative capacity of man grows along with the increase of his consciousness and knowledge.

---

[23] The more developed reflective thinking becomes in man – this large molecule of the energy-unity –, the more will his subjective "knowledge", his conceptions of the universe, its forms and behavior, correspond to objective fact.

The more conscious he becomes, the greater and more comprehensive becomes his power over himself and over the less conscious and still unconscious energy forms.

Priority

The next recognizable goal of evolution is energy's consciousness of itself. On Earth, energy is so far able to become conscious of itself only in human beings, through the capacity for reflective thought that has developed in them. On Earth, human beings, the conscious animals, are consequently the highest forms of life and the most worthy of preservation.

The kind of *pro-evo* behavior which *prevents harm to human beings and furthers them in the best possible way* therefore *has the highest priority*. But not a blade of grass, not a tree, not an animal or other energy form, should be harmed unless absolutely necessary for human life and its evolution.

Wisdom

Furthering the development of oneself, one's fellow men and the rest of the environment in the best possible way, consistently avoiding even the most trivial *anti-evo* thoughts and actions – this is the greatest wisdom.

Will

In the course of his evolution, man has learned that he can best achieve his aims and desires when he concentrates on them without giving up. This knowledge gave rise to conscious will. Will can be applied in both *pro-evo* and *anti-evo* ways.

We should develop wills that enable us to pursue steadfastly our *pro-evo* goals, tasks and behavior and that are far stronger than any *anti-evo* instincts or inclinations.[24]

Conscience

Conscience is "stored experience" of which a person becomes conscious automatically when he is about to make a decision or perform an act important for himself or the environment, or when he is considering the "rightness" or "wrongness" of particular goals, tasks or behavior.

The regulating structures of the human mind which trigger conscience were, like all regulating structures, formed by *pro-evo* and *anti-evo* "experiences". They consequently operate sometimes only partially, and often not at all, in a *pro-evo* way.

Conscience is thus not always a reliable guideline for thought and action. It has already brought mis-

---

[24] Fasting one day a week, for example, helps develop willpower.

fortune and death to countless individuals and peoples.

Therefore, a man should examine his "voice of conscience" thoroughly and *follow it only when he is convinced that it is pro-evo.*

Morality

Morality is man's conscious *pro-evo* behavior toward his own body, toward his fellow men, and toward animals, plants and the natural environment.

Beauty

Beauty is the luster, the radiance, the reflection, of the *pro-evo* in energy forms and in representations of them.

For instance, a man who thinks and acts in a life-promoting way – free of *anti-evo* tensions – radiates harmony, order and joy. We find him beautiful even if his physical features are not harmonious.

Faith

Faith is any conception which appears to the believer as not just probable or possible, but as one whose truth and reality is *unwaveringly certain.* Thoughts undistracted by doubt, which build belief, create regulating structures that strongly influence the conscious and unconscious behavior of the believer.

Strong faith therefore often "works wonders", "moves mountains".

Prophecies

Prophecies, statements and assertions which a person *believes* in, and *does not doubt,* form in him regulating structures which direct his behavior, favoring the occurrence of the predicted events or even actually bringing them about. (This experience shows how important it is to examine critically all the ideas to which we are exposed – in particular, political and commercial propaganda – so that they do not lead to the formation in us of *anti-evo* regulating structures that may interfere with our lives.)

Soul

What is commonly understood by "soul" is a part of the regulating structures, and of the abilities made possible and released by them ("living", feeling, thinking, consciousness, conscience, etc.).

Regulating structures are genetically inherited. If a man has no descendants, his regulating structures are lost finally and irretrievably at his death – even those which constituted his "soul".

(The traditional concept of the immortality of the

human soul is untenable. It contradicts the facts of the evolution of energy. When might man's immortal soul have been created? At what stage of evolution? In the electromagnetic fields, or in the atoms, gases, material substances, in plants, fish, hedgehogs, primates, in Stone Age or Bronze Age man, or when?)[25]

Guilt

Even when a person consciously – deliberately – acts in an *anti-evo* way, he is *innocent.* His regulating structures and environmental influences are responsible for his actions. "Trapped in error", he will not have been able to think or act otherwise.

It is therefore wrong to judge him, punish him or "take retribution". Rather we have a duty to persuade the erring person of the need for *pro-evo* thinking and acting, and to lead him in that direction – and, if necessary, to protect human society effectively from him as long as there is still a risk that he might endanger and harm it.

---

[25] Even important thinkers of the past who did not have the benefit of scientific findings about the evolution of energy, such as Lao Tzu, Confucius and Buddha, "knew" that individual life after death is not possible.

Sin and crime

Whoever committed a sin, burdened himself with guilt – according to traditional ideas – and was led to expect punishment.

Today we know that man's thoughts and actions are primarily the result of the interaction of his regulating structures and environment – and that it would be wrong to pronounce a person guilty because of "sinful" thoughts and deeds or to punish him.

The more inadequate a person's regulating structures and environmental circumstances are, and the worse his "sins" may be, the greater the unhappiness and harm that thus befalls him – and the more deserving of pity and in need of help he is.

In the past the observance of religious and ethical rules was sought to be achieved through threats of punishment in this world and after death – of purgatory, eternal damnation or reincarnation into an animal, etc.

The person who is aware of the Prime Force and its evolution thinks and acts in a *pro-evo* way of his own accord – avoids all *anti-evo,* "sinful" and criminal ideas and deeds – because he knows that only by acting in that way can *joy and well-being* be attained and unhappiness and harm largely prevented. For him any threat of punishment is superfluous, not necessary as a help in his life.

Remorse

Recognition of our past *anti-evo* actions, and our remorse for them – our true regret that we have committed them and our firm resolve to act only *pro-evo* in the future –, apparently have the effect of weakening or erasing the "impressions", the regulating structures, formed by that *anti-evo* behavior. Through our remorse we experience inner liberation; and the firm, unshakeable decision to live in a *pro-evo* way in the future brings our thinking into harmony with the stream of life, cosmic evolution.

Reincarnation

We reincarnate ourselves through the regulating structures contained in our seed cells, which create our children, and also through our thoughts and actions, which influence – "go into" – our children and our other fellow men.

Belief in *a reincarnation after death* is based on erroneous conclusions, which are derived primarily from supposed "memories of earlier lives". These memories, however, originated from events which happened in the lives of our ancestors and which formed in them regulating structures which we inherited.

With death, our existence comes to a definitive end. But in our children and the other fellow men and their descendants, we live on forever – through our germ cells and the effects of our thoughts and actions.

As if led by an invisible force

Our *pro-evo* thoughts and actions and the regulating structures formed by them benefit our lives.

For example: we meet people who are of exceptional help to us; we find advice and books that are right for us; changes that are important for us happen at the right time; we escape natural disasters and accidents due to human error if it is at all possible to do so, etc.

Whoever steadfastly thinks and acts in a *pro-evo* way feels led by an invisible force.

(The explanation may be as follows: man is linked with his environment through countless relationships and connections. Together with them he forms the indivisible, interlinked and interwoven energy-unity, the infinite "network" of the universe. His *pro-evo* thoughts and deeds and the regulating structures formed by them trigger events – actions and reactions – which have *pro-evo* consequences for him, furthering and protecting him.)

Fear

The person who knows he is part of the energy-unity of the universe and thinks and acts in a *pro-evo* way is in harmony with the environment and in tune with the stream of life.

In him energy has become conscious of itself. He is no longer in the "narrowness" of his own small self – and so becomes free of all "fear".

When he nevertheless protects himself from the *anti-evo* acts of his fellow men, he does this not out of fear, but to prevent himself and his *pro-evo* actions from being endangered by the mistakes of others.

Freedom

Through countless ties and influences, human beings, together with all other energy forms, are indivisibly interwoven parts of the universal unity. Their behavior is triggered by their regulating structures, together with the environment; even every so-called *free* choice and action of a person results from these causes.

People are thus *bound, dependent,* cells in the energy organism of the cosmos – therefore *without freedom of thought and action.*

By the term "freedom" as commonly used we understand: to be able to choose – apparently freely and unhindered – between the various possibilities for shaping one's life.

This "*freedom of decision*" is a product of reflective thinking. It can be used in a *pro-evo* or *anti-evo* way. Depending on the particular choice, it has *pro-evo* or *anti-evo* consequences.

People *mis*use their freedom of decision when they choose *anti-evo* goals and behavior. They thereby bring about unhappiness and harm.

Reflective thinking and freedom of decision are essential abilities for the conscious animal – man.

They should be furthered to the fullest possible extent.

The struggle against suppression of freedom of decision for fellow human beings or institutions has made the concept of “freedom” very popular; yet it is often misunderstood. Many people conclude, out of the legitimate demands by the oppressed for freedom of decision, that there is a “universal human right” to do whatever one wants, whatever, for example, best satisfies their desires for possessions, dominance, sex, aggression or comfort. This conclusion is fatal and causes enormous harm. One’s goals and behavior should not be determined by “free”, unrestrained and uninhibited instincts and desires, but should be measured against the *pro-evo principle* alone; otherwise unhappiness and harm are unavoidable. *Constant abuse of the freedom of decision leads to ruin.*

Culture

The term culture means for us *conscious, disciplined, pro-evo behavior and its consequences,* in all their variety.

Steadfastness

Every thought and action affects one’s own body and life as well as one’s environment.

How important it is, therefore, that we be steadfast in our endeavors to think and act only in a *pro-evo* way …

Human worth

A person's worth is determined not by his skin color, race or religion, or by the social class he comes from – nor by his social position, power or possessions, nor by his physical or intellectual abilities or the way he has developed them – but *solely by the intensity and persistence of his endeavors to think and act in a pro-evo way.*

Masters of life

People who consciously and steadfastly think and act in a *pro-evo* way are the masters of life.

Resolutely, energetically, unceasingly, rapidly, carefully, kindly, without force – and without avoidably harming their fellow men and the rest of the environment – they pursue their *pro-evo* goals and tasks, as heads of state, nurses, scientists, housewives, astronauts and so on.

They are the noble ones.

Constant, conscious improvement – the real task of mankind

The stream of life develops, intensifies, regenerates and improves without ceasing …

It would therefore be *anti-evo* to be satisfied with, or even cling to, an existing state of affairs.

The real task of mankind is the conscious pro-evo development of everything that has been achieved in all areas of life – education, the development of intellectual capacity and consciousness, nutrition, clothing, housing, relationships between people and the relationship of people to their environment, etc.

Question everything, improve everything; hourly, daily, without delay or hesitation, make all that now exists more pro-evo.

("Progress" that is *not directed and controlled in a pro-evo way* can cause avoidable harm or even endanger or destroy parts or the whole of mankind. For this reason it is imperative that scientific research, in particular, and the application of its results, be conducted strictly according to the *pro-evo principle* in order to avoid any detrimental effects, or to at least keep them within safe and tolerable limits – safe even from human error and technical failings.)

Human society

The union of mankind

Once *pro-evo* love – the conscious furthering of other people – has become a commonly felt need, people will be united and immense forces that were formerly absorbed by people fighting one another will be freed, benefiting all areas of life to a hitherto unimagined extent.

Working together

Those who practice *pro-evo* love, that is, those who want to further other people, will develop their inherited abilities in the best possible way and endeavor to apply their acquired skills to the maintenance and development of human society.

Individuals, groups, races and states who strive only for their own well-being, without showing consideration for human society as a whole or contributing to it in the way they should, are acting in a parasitic, anti-life way.

Why can conscious people never be disappointed by their fellow human beings?

Conscious people further others as best they can – without thereby jeopardizing the *pro-evo* quality of their own existence – and do not expect thanks or any other specific form of behavior in return. They have a positive attitude toward others as they are, with all their potential for both *pro-evo* and *anti-evo* thoughts and actions, and are tolerant of their faults.

Conscious people are therefore never disappointed by their fellow human beings.

Choosing a life partner

People whose intellectual capacity and consciousness are inadequately developed choose their life partner on the basis of certain instincts: for example, strong sexual attraction or satisfaction of their laziness or urge to dominate.

People with good intelligence and clear consciousness choose life partners who endeavor to think and act *pro-evo* or who can in all probability be led to do so through explanation.

People who think and act *pro-evo* will consciously love their life partners and will constantly further them – not just for as long as the physical attraction remains strong, and even if they separate and enter into new relationships.

How is lasting happiness through love achieved?

Happiness in love is preserved by the conscious furthering of one's partner – through giving, helping, explaining, forgiving – and through the feeling and knowledge that we are one with our partner and that with him or her we form, together with the environment, the indivisible unity of the universe.

Courage and watchfulness

We should cheerfully and fearlessly pursue our *pro-evo* goals and tasks, and never deviate from them, even under the influence of the opinions, flattery or criticism of other people or of supposed advantages or disadvantages – but be watchful "so that no one trapped in error strikes us from behind".

Winning agreement

Approval or agreement cannot be achieved by force. But people agree with *pro-evo* goals and tasks and help in their accomplishment when these are *clearly explained.*

"… like grass before the wind"

If we steadfastly think and act *pro-evo*, then one day most people within our influence will follow our lead "like grass before the wind".

Friends

We should seek the company of people who consistently strive to think and act *only pro-evo*, who can help us and whom we can help to achieve better self-control.

Enemies

Even our enemies – people who wish or do us harm – should be loved, i. e., furthered and helped to recognize that they are part of the universal unity and therefore harm even themselves – their true "selves" – when they act in an *anti-evo* way.

Enemies whom we further will usually sooner or later give up their hostile behavior or vanish from our lives.

Conflict

"Conflict is fighting one's fellow human beings."

We should search for solutions that are *pro-evo* and fair to all parties when faced with differences or conflicts, and persistently, calmly, objectively, courteously and benevolently endeavor to win our opponents' agreement.

All differences can be resolved through *pro-evo* synthesis.

Forgive

We should answer the harm that others have done us with *pro-evo* behavior – and protect ourselves effectively from any further damage at their hands.

Forgive, pardon – establish untroubled relationships with other people.

Show solidarity

Understanding and kindness, and a sympathetic, man-to-man approach to other people should be the rule, and not cold, harsh or even cynical words.

We should let people feel that we know ourselves to be indivisibly united with them in the universal unity, always emphasize what is shared and unifying and put our differences in the background.

Acknowledge achievements

Acknowledge the achievements of other people, do not belittle or conceal them. Strengthen their self-confidence so that they achieve even greater things.

The great majority of people want what is pro-evo

The overwhelming majority of people support, consciously and unconsciously, *pro-evo* ideas and actions.

Illness as a result of the absence of pro-evo goals

Many "sick" people, including all depressives, are lacking in a *pro-evo* attitude towards existence. They can see no goals that are worth living for.

As soon as they realize that the world – including their own bodies – is the everlasting energy unity and that they will be joyful and happy when they think and act in a *pro-evo* way, they begin to recover from their illness.

And they will completely overcome their poor psychological state when they are helped to find and achieve their *pro-evo* goals and tasks – those which further themselves, their fellow men and their surroundings.

Instructions and requests

Comply with the instructions and requests of other people only when these serve *pro-evo* goals and tasks. Refuse to comply when you know the instructions and requests would have *anti-evo* effects.

Conscious and unconscious pro-evo behavior towards others

If we love our fellow men – further them, wish and help bring about for them what is *pro-evo* – corresponding regulating structures will be formed in us; and even our unconscious behavior towards them will become *pro-evo.*

We need not then be surprised when we are furthered by other people – though probably not always by the ones to whom we have shown the most love.

Through the pro-evo, overcome and hold away the anti-evo

The individual person and every social group – family, local community, state, etc. – should overcome and keep at bay what is *anti-evo* by *persistently striving to bring about the pro-evo.* (People should be guided towards the *pro-evo* goals and tasks of their community by means of simple, easily understandable guidelines.)

Be careful where there is a lot of talk

When the goals and tasks are *pro-evo*, there is no need for a lot of talk to win people over to them. Therefore, where there is a lot of talk, be careful.

Like-minded people

We should work together with like-minded people in order to recognize both our own and society's *pro-evo* goals and tasks more clearly and achieve them more quickly.

Support and direction for human society

Those who persistently think and act in a *pro-evo* way will "permeate" human society to an increasing extent and give it support and direction.

The role of women

Consciously-thinking women will in the future have a role in human society equal to that of men and fully appropriate to their sex. They will defend everything that is life-promoting, often more resolutely and energetically than men. And they will approve of and respect the ideas and actions of men only when these promote life.

Differences in the way we shape our lives

People, their inherited regulating structures (their physical, psychological, and intellectual "constitution"), their education and training, the influence of the environment, their will and self-control, are all different from one another. As a result, even when they have the same opportunities for shaping their lives, they will perceive and exploit them in quite different ways.

How important is humanity?

The evolution of present-day mankind and our immediate predecessors took twenty million years, and for billions of years to come human beings or beings similar to us will be able to live on this planet.

In this time who knows how often the human species could vanish – through its own fault or through destruction by giant meteors, cosmic radiation, etc. – and how often new species with reflective intelligence could develop, even if the new development were to take somewhat longer.

A dangerous phase in human evolution

The progress of science in the twentieth century led to the production of means of destruction – atom bombs, chemical and biological weapons, missiles – with which human existence on Earth could be severely harmed or even completely destroyed.

The behavior of many political leaders is unfortunately still strongly influenced by aggression, possessiveness, a striving for dominance and other desires, instincts and fears – of which they are broadly unaware. Therefore, the acute danger exists that these terrible modern means of destruction will be used for reasons of power and greed, or as a result of unjustified fears or other *anti-evo* causes and motives.

Leading positions in government should therefore be given only to people who are convinced that *pro-evo thought and action are imperative* and who can be expected to behave steadfastly in a corresponding manner in all situations and at all times.

Only if pro-evo thought and action is allowed to dominate politics can the extensive or even complete destruction of our human race by modern weaponry be avoided.

Population growth and abortion

The laws governing abortion should not be allowed to obscure the general prohibition against killing – since its function is to protect life in society.

For this reason, abortion should not be used as a means of population control. Instead, only methods that prevent excess pregnancies, such as late marriage, contraception, or temporary sterilization, etc. should be used for this purpose.

Abortion should be permitted only when a woman becomes pregnant against the *express will* of one or both of the partners or when, during a wanted pregnancy, circumstances become known or develop which would make carrying the baby to full term senseless, such as serious danger to the health of mother or child; or where the pregnancy and birth would result in an unusual degree of social or material hardship for the parents. The termination of pregnancy where the health of the mother or child is at risk should be allowed at any time, whereas in other cases it should be limited to the period when the embryo is still at the pre-human stage of development – when it is not yet a "person".

(In order to prevent parents from making a wrong decision – as a result, for example, of inadequate information about help available in the community or about the physical and psychological effects of an abortion – a discussion with authorized parent counsellors should be made mandatory. Further, in the event of an abortion, it should be mandatory to have the operation performed by a qualified medical professional.)

How many people should live on our planet?

As many people should inhabit the Earth as can live on it in a *pro-evo* way – no more, but no fewer either.

What does the *pro-evo* existence of mankind entail? Air, water, nutrition, clothing and housing that are not harmful to health; adequate opportunities for exercise; education and training by the most effective methods, etc.

Why shouldn't fewer people inhabit the Earth? The more people that live on Earth in the right living conditions, the greater is the likelihood of *mankind's evolving in the shortest and best way.*[26]

Which countries or organizations will inherit the leadership of the peoples of our planet?

The leadership of the peoples of our planet will pass peacefully to those countries or organizations which clearly recognize, make known and strive to realize the *pro-evo* goals of mankind.

What does the continuance of human social orders depend on?

All human social orders without *pro-evo* love – without striving to further mankind – do not last.

Leaders

The more important the positions of leaders, their advisers and other influential people in society – the larger the number of people whose destiny they af-

---

[26] Scientists, politicians and economists who think and act in a *pro-evo* way will – if they are given the opportunity – provide optimal living conditions at every stage of human development. People who think and act in an *anti-life* way are not usually capable of doing so, and in growth and economic situations which, as a consequence of their lack of creativity, they consider hopeless, they spread an atmosphere of doom and instigate correspondingly negative measures. In positions of leadership such people often do untold harm to entire nations.

fect – the more necessary it is that they think and act solely in a *pro-evo* way.

People who *consciously* act in an *anti-evo* way or are incompetent do not belong in leading or influential positions in the community, region or state, in the economy, in administration or in the arts, etc.

The responsibility of leaders

Leaders should be held responsible for any damage they do as a result of their *incompetent, negligent* or *consciously anti-evo* decisions and actions.

Education

Are people born good or bad?

At birth people are endowed with regulating structures that are partly *pro-evo*, partly *anti-evo*, and in the course of life these will be reinforced or weakened through education, other environmental influences and personal effort and behavior.

The most important tasks of schools

To educate young people to think and act in a *pro-evo* way, and develop their consciousness and ability to think to the extent that their inherited regulating structures permit, is the most important task of schools. *Pro-evo* forms of behavior such as self-control, love of others, prudence, initiative, orderliness, cleanliness, decency and punctuality, should be developed by means, for example, of repeated practical exercises.[27]

Continuing education

The constant development of our intellectual capacity and consciousness and the increase of our knowledge are essential to the shaping of our lives.

Only in this way will we be able to recognize with increasing accuracy the *pro-evo* goals and tasks in all areas of our lives and become better at choosing and applying the means of achieving them.

Self-control

Discipline – the constant control of behavior, thought and action – is essential.

Without firm self-control we cannot satisfactorily realize our *pro-evo* goals and tasks. Without discipline our lives run on like "idle chatter".

---

[27] The rapid growth of mankind's knowledge and technical abilities, which we can expect to continue in the future, will be paralleled by an explosive increase in the danger of self-destruction and chaos unless it can permanently be instilled into people that their knowledge and ability should be used only in a *pro-evo* – life-promoting – way.

Some pro-evo principles for bringing up children

Teach children about *pro-evo* thought and action, which produce joy and happiness, and about *anti-evo* thought and action, which produce unhappiness and harm.

Encourage children to examine constantly their own behavior and that of others – including those bringing them up – to determine whether it is *pro-evo.*

Teach children *pro-evo* love of others (helpfulness, consideration, forgiveness of wrongs done to them, courtesy, gratitude, etc.). But also explain to them that they must reject and protect themselves from the *anti-evo* behavior of others.

Let children constantly learn through experience that self-control, cleanliness, decency and orderliness are indispensable for the health and fitness of the body and for social existence.

Give children *pro-evo* tasks that benefit their social environment (the family, etc.) from an early age and teach them to accomplish these *sensibly* and *energetically.*

Set children high standards of achievement and give them every encouragement.

Love children without reservation, even when they do not behave as we would like. And guide them towards *pro-evo* behavior with patience and kindness.

Children must be able to rely on us absolutely. They must know and see every day that we support *pro-evo* and reject *anti-evo* behavior.

Firm guidance

So long as children and adolescents have not developed sufficient independent judgement, and lack the knowledge and experience needed to recognize and adopt the *pro-evo* behavior necessary for their own development and for their relationships with their surroundings, they need *firm* – but kind and patient – guidance.

For parents, guardians and schools to neglect such guidance in *pro-evo* thought and action is not only wrong but is a *serious human failure.*

Protest and duty

Young people often protest against grownups merely in order to shirk their "duty".

What is their "duty"? To conduct themselves in a *pro-evo* – life-promoting – way in every situation.

Good and bad examples

A person's behavior and his portrayal of modes of behavior imprint in his fellow men regulating structures that influence their future behavior.

This explains the beneficial effect of "good" examples and the detrimental effect of "bad" ones.

The less conscious a person is, then the less inhibited by doubt and criticism he is, and as a result there are more directly and strongly imprinted in him regulating structures which influence his future behavior. For this reason children, adolescents and uncritical adults should never, for example, be exposed to *anti-evo* behavior on television, in movies, on the radio, on the stage or in print without simultaneously having it made clear to them that – and for what reasons – this is *anti-evo* and hence to be rejected.

Lack of discipline

People whose behavior is undisciplined and uncontrolled should be restrained firmly by society as long as they are not capable of controlling themselves and endanger or harm their environment with their *anti-evo* behavior.

Psychoanalysis and behavioral therapy

Revealing the origins of *anti-evo* behavior ("wrong behavior") is certainly important in understanding the psychological context and its effects. But by that alone *anti-evo* behavior cannot be overcome.

Anti-evo behavior can be eliminated only when the regulating structures which cause it are erased and replaced by *pro-evo* regulating structures. Regulating structures are, as we know, formed and destroyed through conscious and unconscious learning (experience, conditioning).

Therefore, all we need to do in order to free people from their wrong behavior is:

(1) make it clear to them that the regulating structures – the guiding programs and mechanisms

that trigger and determine their *anti-evo* thoughts and actions – are in part inherited and in part formed through the experience of their own bodies and through environmental influences, the most lasting regulating structures being those that developed in the first five years of their life;

(2) explain to them the *pro-evo* behavior they should strive for in order to overcome their wrong behavior; and

(3) help them to achieve this *pro-evo* behavior systematically, step by step.

To overcome wrong behavior, research into the hereditary and environmental origins of the regulating structures producing it is not necessary.[28]

Art

Works of art

There should be considered as works of art only works by *artists* – masters of music, poetry, sculpture, painting, dance, etc. – that:

(1) represent the *pro-evo*, or

---

[28] Compare, for example, *H. J. Eysenck* "You and Neurosis".

(2) represent the *anti-evo* but with the *aim* to promote or accomplish the overcoming of the *anti-evo.*[29]

Misuse of artistic talents

The representation of the *anti-evo* without *pro-evo* aim – without the intention of thereby overcoming it – is misuse of the artist's special abilities, and will cloud or even choke the springs of his talent.

The effect of an art work

An art work affects us through its *pro-evolutionness.* If we "observe it with feeling and understanding", we experience agreeably its harmony with the stream of life in us.

The future of art

Up now, the *pro-evo* in art has been portrayed for the most part unconsciously. The artists of the future will express it consciously in their works.

Perhaps a new dawn in art will break soon.

[29] Compare, for example, similar comments by modern painters such as *Henri Matisse*, *Vasili Kandinsky*, *Max Beckmann* and *Max Ernst.*

Law

The only valid standard for law and its interpretation

The *pro-life principle* alone is the only valid standard for law and its interpretation.

Bring justice, *pro-life-ness*, to be the ruling principle everywhere – without compromise.

The explanation of laws

As soon as people understand the *pro-evo* principle of laws – their correspondence with the requirements of human life – they obey them. Therefore the laws should be fully explained and justified.

When laws and orders are not heeded by mentally healthy people with normal intelligence, then these laws or orders are either *anti-evo* or have been insufficiently explained.

In order to protect society, psychologically unstable and psychiatrically ill people should be deterred from breaking the law by the threat of tough enforcement measures.

Lawbreakers

People who with *anti-evo* behavior harm other people or their environment beyond what is tolerable – the lawbreakers – should required to make good as far as possible the damage they have done, should be educated in *pro-evo* behavior and should if necessary be kept in "custody" until it is unlikely that they will in the future endanger or harm other people.

The education of lawbreakers in *pro-evo* behavior is just as important a social duty as educating and training children in schools and requires appropriately trained psychologists and guardians.[30]

Gaps in legislation

Legislation is often too slowly adapted to new needs arising out of social, scientific, technical or economic developments.

For example, we still lack tough measures that effectively deter enticement to consume nicotine, alcohol, narcotics or addictive drugs, or the infliction of intolerable damage on the environment – all of which harm the persons affected to a much greater extent than does, for example, theft or robbery of material goods, for which the punishment is severe.

The economy

What is the task of the economy?

The task of the economy is to create *living conditions* – goods, housing, services, environmental factors, etc. – that *further mankind in the best possible way.*

---

[30] See "Guilt" above in this Part III.

Economic guidance

The more people on Earth, and the more rapid the social, scientific and technological progress, the more indispensable is the establishment of *pro-evo economic goals and behavior*, constantly adjusted to changing circumstances. Without guidelines of that kind, which must be binding on everyone involved in the economy, severe damage to the human community is unavoidable.[31]

How much should economic freedom be restricted?

The freedom – the "individual initiative" – of business persons and organizations should be restricted only to the extent necessary for the assur-

---

[31] Examples of the effect of a lack of *pro-evo* economic guidance:
(1) The unrestrained expansion of the oil and automobile industries after the Second World War, which led, among other things, to the neglect both of mass transportation and of research into, and use of, solar and geothermal energy and other inexhaustible and renewable sources of power, as well as having led in some areas to life-threatening pollution and poisoning of the air, water and soil.
(2) The operation of atomic power plants, and the production of poisons and viruses, that could destroy part or all of mankind – as a result of human failure or technical defects, *which can never be wholly excluded.* (Mankind has experienced time and again that misfortunes that can happen, will happen …)

ance and realization of *pro-evo* economic goals and behavior.

Any further restriction disturbs, obstructs – is *anti-evo* – because it unnecessarily limits the potential of business persons for development and operations.

How could anti-evo economic behavior be prevented?

Almost all *anti-evo* – life-damaging – behavior and conditions in the economy could be prevented *very simply: by making individuals, enterprises, and institutions in the business world strictly responsible for any damage they may cause deliberately or through incompetence or neglect.*

Damage caused by the business world

Some examples of *anti-evo* behavior in the economy:

The manufacture and promotion of goods and services *that do not contribute toward a pro-evo existence or that damage people's health, impair their consciousness or have other anti-evo effects*, such as: food with traces of poisonous weed killers, insecticides or preservatives; pharmaceutical products which remove only the symptoms but not the causes of illness, or result in other illness or damage; narcotics and addictive drugs for non-medical purposes; tobacco products, with their nicotine content; chemical products, which cannot be recycled in nature and are a constant burden on the environment; unhealthy housing; spreading false information (distortion of news, suppression or biased presentation of facts, inadequate or tendentious criticism) leading to misinterpretation of events and situations; forms of entertainment that brutalize or frighten; corruption of the sex drive through the printed word or pictures, with the danger of leading to behavior damaging to the body, mind or society; poisoning of the environment by radiation, gases or other material; built-in obsolescence in manufactured products; delaying the application of findings or inventions which could improve goods, services or environmental conditions; setting unjust prices, interest rates or wages; speculation in raw materials or other goods; all other forms of manipulation of production, supply and demand to the detriment of human society; and so on.

Import-export

The importing of goods – merchandise and other – is of economic benefit to the importing economy only when thereby a current emergency is met or a lasting improvement in living conditions is achieved – which was achievable only by that means.

The importing of goods that could be produced domestically in sufficient quality and amount weakens the economy unnecessarily. The weakening comes from the capital outflow for the goods and *above all from the loss of the stimulus* that domestic production would have given by chain reaction to all parts of the economy.

The importing of such goods is reasonable and acceptable only insofar as it makes possible exports of about the same economic countervalue (compared to what would have been export sale proceeds and other benefits – economic stimulus – from domestic production).[32]

The importing and exporting of goods that in any way harm people – that are *anti-evo* – are absolutely to be stopped; violators are to be held responsible.

Inventions and other innovations

Life-promoting innovations – inventions, know-how, etc. – should be made available *without delay* under appropriate license from all concerned, so as to benefit as many people as possible as soon as possible.

Work

By "work" we mean all activities of people in researching, developing or achieving *pro-life* goals

[32] The debilitating effect of imports without counterbalancing exports can be seen, for example, in the unfavorable development of economic strength in the USA after the Second World War. During that time the USA lost millions of jobs and billions of dollars in the steel, auto, chemical, electronic, retailing, construction and other industries through the loss of production-stimulus alone.

and tasks for themselves, society or the environment.

All work that *can be carried out by machines* should be transferred to them, so that people are free for activities involving creativity, initiative, research, planning and direction, as well as for activities in which human contact is particularly important – education, care of children and the sick, in schools and continued education, in the household, in the service of guests, etc.

The full division of work in this way – between people and machines – will be possible only when, through the intensive use of solar and geothermal energy, among other things, unlimited power is available everywhere to run machines, and when people have reached a level of development enabling them to avoid damage to themselves and society from having too much free time.

We should *carefully train and keep up to date* for work through which, on the basis of our abilities and inclinations, we can best promote our own development and that of the community; and to the extent possible we should accept or undertake work that accords with our knowledge and abilities.

All work should be *planned precisely and carried out as perfectly as possible* – for the good of both the individual and society.

A person who *does no work to maintain himself and makes no appropriate contribution* to *society* – though healthy enough and not of retirement age – or who *does not try to do his work in the best possible way,* behaves like a *parasite,* is a burden to society.

Work must leave a person enough *free time* for adequate relaxation and for self-realization[33] through continuing education, artistic and sporting activity, meditation, and so forth.

Compensation for work should be in proportion to the performance rendered (measured by: initiative, creativity, responsibility, knowledge and know-how, perfection of the work, psychological and physical stress involved, and working hours). The lowest wage must be sufficient to provide working people and their families with adequate food, clothing, housing, health and old age security, as well as optimal upbringing, education and continuing education.

For decades to come, some 1.500 working hours a year from every adult (until retirement) will be necessary in order to create for everyone on Earth, through a cybernetic plan to be commonly agreed upon, the living conditions that, with the help of modern knowledge and capabilities, are desirable and achievable.

Economic development

Economic development is almost completely directable. It is in no way governed by inevitable fate.

The moment *pro-evo* goals and behavior predominate in the economy, it will become crisis-free and create constantly improving living conditions. *The sole causes of economic difficulties* – aside from nat-

[33] Self-realization is *conscious, pro-evo* direction and fulfillment of one's own life.

ural and technical disasters – *are anti-evo economic goals and behavior.*

How could living conditions be improved constantly?

(1) In the various economic regions (countries, etc.) let qualified, *pro-evo* thinking representatives from all sectors of society (scientists, artists, experts from government, business, administration and consumers, etc.) research and plan goals for the improvement of living conditions in all areas of life – starting from existing conditions and having regard to anticipated long-term development.

(2) Initiate at the appropriate time measures necessary to achieve these new goals by, among other things, redirecting human and material resources (land, minerals, factories, tools, machinery, money) from obsolete goals to new ones.[34]

(3) In order not to delay achievement of the new goals, society – which will benefit from the timely changes – should bear the costs of any

---

[34] An example of success of a collective search for the optimal direction of an economy is the meteoric rise of Japan's steel, automobile, camera, watch and electronics industries after the Second World War; as a result of the constant joint *planning* efforts of MITI (Ministry of Trade and Industry) and KEIDANREN (an organization of representatives of industry, banks, science, etc.).

necessary retraining of people, as well as any losses resulting when investments in obsolete goals can no longer be amortized.

The most striking example of constant improvement in people's living conditions – of an increasing "prosperity" and a "flourishing economy" – as a result of realizing *pro-evo* goals is the reconstruction of a country after the ravages of war, often in spite of what appear to be totally inadequate means.

Examples of contemporary, *pro-evo*, economic goals and tasks for industrialized countries – ones that are only slightly less important than reconstruction of war damage – are:

(1) Comprehensive basic and continuing education for everyone by carefully trained teachers and with the help of the most progressive teaching methods and materials (educational films, teaching machines, teaching and experimental workshops, etc.).[35]

(2) Reorienting agriculture to the production of foods without the use of weed killers, insecticides or other substances or methods which damage people's health and endanger the future usability of the ground for cultivation and water conservation.[36]

---

[35] Countries which do not adopt such policies will soon lose much of their economic power, insofar as it is based on scientific research and technology.

[36] As a result, many town dwellers would resettle in rural areas, resulting in a better distribution of the population.

(3) Converting residential areas into healthy, comfortable and humane places, free of air and water pollution and harmful noise, divided into administrative districts of manageable size, and with streets and squares thronged once again with people and not noisy machines spreading poisonous exhaust fumes (as, for example, could in towns be achieved in part through transportation of people and goods by electrically powered vehicles and by limiting private cars).

(4) Replacing outdated housing with new housing that has a positive influence on the health and well-being of the residents; building sufficient numbers of modern nursery schools, retirement homes and community centers.

(5) Constructing new traffic and transportation systems to make journeys between home, work and recreational areas shorter, healthier and more enjoyable.

(6) Providing the best possible facilities for health promotion and sickness care for all citizens (including building recreational and sports facilities in the mountains and by the sea and woods, as well as a sufficient number of hospitals and convalescent homes).

(7) Optimal development of crime prevention systems; building humane prisons; educating lawbreakers about *pro-evo* thought and action; confining lawbreakers until they are no longer likely to endanger or harm other people.

(8) Utilizing in the most effective way solar and geothermal energy and other inexhaustible and renewable energy sources, so as, for example, to replace oil with hydrogen and electricity for powering automobiles, airplanes and other means of transport and for heating residential and industrial buildings.

(9) Eliminating those production facilities (atomic power plants, factories producing poisonous substances, etc.) and materials (atom bombs, poisons, etc.) which could, as a result of human error or technical failure, severely harm and even partially or completely destroy mankind.[37]

(10) The comprehensive *pro-evo* application of the then most advanced technologies in all sectors of the economy, in industry, agriculture, management, etc.

(11) The establishment of a research organization for monitoring the effect of scientific and technical innovations on man and the environment; and for working for, and enforcing, measures to prevent *anti-evo* consequences from the innovations.

The realization of *pro-life* goals and tasks can always be financed. There are reliable methods and

---

[37] See "Constant, conscious improvement – the real task of mankind" above in this Part III.

measures for preventing both shortage of capital and risk of currency depreciation.[38]

An economic system that serves people in a pro-evo way knows no crises. It achieves ever new *pro-evo* goals for the improvement of human existence.

An economy that is guided in a *pro-evo* way has a constant *shortage of labor,* because the tasks that must be accomplished for the good of mankind are countless.

Leading, authoritative statesmen, politicians, management experts, business people (employees and employers) who, through inability or for other *anti-evo* reasons, delay or even prevent timely research into and realization of *pro-evo* economic goals and tasks for the particular time – and thereby the constant betterment of people's living conditions – must be replaced with more capable persons.[39]

---

[38] For example:
(1) Binding guidelines for fixing prices, wages and interest rates; and
(2) Loans with long-terms, low interest rates and repayment schedules based on average earnings.

[39] As a result of the turbulent growth of scientific knowledge and technical possibilities and the strong increase in world population, faulty economic developments cannot be prevented by means of previous economic methods – even less than in the past. *Now and in the future the economy needs to be managed in a pro-evo life way by the most capable people in the community.* Only with permanent *pro-evo* goal-setting and work toward the goals, which must be binding for all in business, can immeasurable disadvantages and dangers to society, disorder and destruction be avoided. (*Pro-evo* goals and

Material possessions

We should treat the possessions that we earn or are given to us as held in trust to administer and use for the purpose of leading a *pro-evo* existence, in particular for the education, development and expansion of both our own consciousness and that of persons within our sphere of influence.

The collecting and hoarding of goods that are not used for *pro-evo* purposes – not even to provide in a *pro-evo* way for our own future and that of the people we are responsible for – is a thoughtless or pathological form of behavior.[40]

Death

What does man most want to prevent from dying?

Man is primarily concerned with preserving his consciousness. The body is to him the means by which he can live consciously.

---

guidelines do not prevent business people, enterprises or institutions from acting on their own initiative. Such goals and guidelines serve only to set certain limits on goals and behavior in order to ensure that economic progress is made and that human living conditions are constantly improved. Within these limits, *personal initiative is in no way restricted and is worthy of every encouragement.*)

[40] See "*Best living conditions*" under "Living in joy" in Part II above.

In order to preserve consciousness from final extinction, most people would be prepared to replace incurably diseased organs of their bodies, and – if it were possible – to transplant their healthy brains from their dying or hopelessly damaged bodies into healthy bodies with incurably damaged brains.

Immortality – a utopia?

Man will cease dying of old age – this will no longer be necessary for human evolution – only when he has reached such a high level of consciousness that his further development would proceed more rapidly and efficiently without death. At this level of consciousness he will have succeeded not only in preserving his brain and other physical organs but also in continually perfecting them.

However, as long as man's consciousness is below this level, evolution through birth and death, the development of people with a constant succession of new gene combinations – genotypes – will continue.

Suicide

As long as a person's reflective thinking does not completely fail, there remains the possibility of his thinking and acting in a *pro-evo* way for himself and his environment, thus performing the *pro-evo* for the energy unity of the universe. Suicide is therefore just as *anti-evo* as murder or capital punishment.

Suicide is usually the result of a lack of perspective to see all the alternatives and possibilities for action that life has to offer in every situation. People who consciously think and act in a *pro-evo* way will never consider a premature voluntary death, unless unbearable, unpreventable pain renders further living meaningless.

Unconsciousness – a state free from pain and suffering

Our consciousness will be extinguished by death, as in a dreamless sleep, or when we faint or are under an anaesthetic. Normally we experience the fading of our consciousness at least once every 24 hours. We know from this daily experience that the state of unconsciousness is free from pain and suffering.

Overcoming the fear of death

As soon as man recognizes himself as a concentration of energy particles within the everlasting energy unity of the universe and thinks and acts in a *pro-evo* way – *as soon as the energy unity becomes conscious of itself in him* – his fear of death vanishes.

But nevertheless he will do everything to preserve his existence to the utmost biological limit so that he can think and act *pro-evo* – further the evolution of energy forms – for as long as possible and live in *joy*.

The *energy* of the particles to which man owes his existence – which constitute his body and which, in part during his life and in part after his death, in changed forms leave him – is *everlasting*. As evolution continues, this energy will participate in the development of ever more conscious beings and ultimately in absolute consciousness ...[41]

Is there a super-cosmos, a "God"?

The mental ability and knowledge of today's man permits still no complete answer. Moreover, the possible existence of a super-cosmos is of no importance for the goals and behavior of man.

Supposing there is a super-cosmos that had created our cosmos – the energy and the motivational evolution-principle – out of itself: then everything *pro-evo* in our cosmos would also be that in the "sense" of the super-cosmos; and our thoughts and actions that harmonize with cosmic evolution would also thereby be wholly in harmony with the super-cosmos.

Therefore, through our *pro-evo* thinking and acting *joy* arises in us and our lives unfold in the best possible way – whether or not there is a super-cosmos (or even a super-super-cosmos, etc.).

---

[41] See "*What is the next recognizable goal of the evolution of the universe?*" under "Consciousness" above in this Part III.

Some questions for weekly examination of one's own behavior

> *"If I think and act in a pro-evo way, I feel joyful and my life follows the best possible course."*
>
> *"If I think and act in an anti-evo way, I am endangered at every turn and my life is without joy."*

Have I set *pro-evo* goals for my health (moderate diet – vegetarian insofar as practicable –, clothing and housing that are not debilitatingly luxurious, daily physical exercise, etc.), my pursuit of further knowledge, my relationships with other people and my contribution to society?

Do I, every new day and in every new situation, establish the *pro-evo* tasks that I should be carrying out for my own good, the good of others and the good of the rest of my environment?

Do I plan the measures and the allocation of time and resources needed in order to achieve my goals and carry out my tasks in the best possible way?

Do I carry out the measures necessary for the pursuit of my goals and tasks resolutely, rapidly, energetically, prudently, carefully and unceasingly?

Do my *pro-evo* activities succeed one another without interruption (work, recreation, pursuit of further knowledge, meditation, etc.)?

Do I have my basic instincts under control, so that they affect my life and surroundings only in a positive way?

Do I avoid habits as soon as they have anti-life consequences?

Am I unwaveringly truthful in word and deed (without unnecessarily causing pain)?

Do I avoid talking unnecessarily? Do I put my *pro-evo* point of view in a few words and then keep quiet?

Do I treat my material possessions as held in trust to administer and use for *pro-evo* purposes?

Do I strive for order and *pro-evo* conditions in all areas of my life?

Do I love my fellow human beings – in other words, do I further them and never harm them? Do I treat them, even enemies and ingrates, warmly and with good will?

Do I, however, firmly reject the *anti-evo* goals and behavior of other people and organizations (countries, associations, businesses, etc.) and warn against them – without causing offence?

Do I help other people and organizations discover their *pro-evo* goals and behavior, by offering them my opinion and explaining my reasons for it?

Do I avoid wasting energy, time or resources on people who – with sufficient personal effort – could also help themselves?

Do I follow instructions and comply with requests of other people only when I am convinced that these are *pro-evo*?

Is my conduct courteous, reserved, tactful and straightforward?

Am I, when conflict arises, especially accommodating, tolerant and helpful? In the case of conflicts or differences, do I attempt to find *pro-evo* solutions and try with patience and good will to win agreement?

Do I *recognize* the achievements of others? Do I encourage them to go on to even greater achievements?

Do I help bring competent people, who think and act in *pro-evo* ways, to positions of leadership in society?

Do I consistently avoid surrounding myself with things that hinder and put a strain on my development – my life?

Do I strive *steadfastly* and wholeheartedly to achieve goals, tasks and behavior I recognize as *pro-evo*? Do I resist being dissuaded from them by the criticism, flattery or ridicule of other people, or by supposed personal advantages or disadvantages?

Suggestions for readers who would like to meditate occasionally on themes from this book

Lie on your back – your arms by your sides, palms down – or sit in a relaxed position with a straight back, preferably in a yoga position.

With closed lids, direct your eyes towards the, center of your forehead and relax them completely.

Concentrate on your breathing, observing how the body inhales and exhales through the nose.

Once your breathing is regular, visualize the theme on which you want to meditate in all its detail;

consider it from all angles and observe all the thoughts that "enter your head" in this context. The meditation can be continued for as long as desired.

After meditating on the chosen theme, concentrate on your breathing again for a few minutes and then stand up.

Some suggested themes for meditation

"I am a conscious 'cell' of the infinite energy organism of the universe – the universal unity."

"The evolution-drive vibrates in me and in all other energy forms of the universe."

"When my thoughts and action are in tune with the life stream, when they are *pro-evo* – life-promoting – joy arises in me and my life unfolds in the best possible way."

"If my ideas and actions are not in tune with the stream of life, if they are *anti-evo* – harmful to life –, I am endangered at every turn and without joy."

"For all areas of life and every situation I will establish my *pro-evo* goals and modes of behavior and put all my energies into achieving them."

"The realization that *the energy of the universe is my true self* and that *the pro-evo principle is the unfailing guideline for my thoughts and actions to produce joy and happiness* gives me a completely new feeling of life: I have clarity, security and vigor as never before."

Epilogue

Answers to often-asked questions:

(1) *Why does the author claim that Friedrich Nietzsche's theory of "eternal recurrence" cannot be true?*

Because the only cosmic certainties are the universal unity and that its energy forms constantly change, never rest and will never be alike.

(2) *In what way does the pro-evo ethic differ fundamentally from other ethical systems, such as Aristotle's, etc.?*

The *pro-evo ethic* is based primarily on the reflection that (a) the energy forms – human beings and their environment – are inseparably connected with one another and constitute the organism of the universe, (b) the energy forms – *as a whole* – are continuously evolving, and (c) therefore *our thinking and acting can be right only when it is directed in the same direction* as this overall evolution, *when it furthers our own evolution and that of our environment and prevents avoidable harm.*

To Aristotle, for example, slavery was perfectly "good" and "natural". He probably never thought it should be abolished. At best he argued for better treatment of slaves, for economic reasons or perhaps because he felt a nascent sympathy for these "man-like beings".

Absolutely unacceptable for *pro-evo* thinking persons are: the enslavement of people; or the guiding principles of other ethical systems which likewise tolerate or sometimes even require *the nonfurthering and the avoidable-harming of people.*

(3) *Is there proof of the effect of thoughts on nonhuman forms of life?*

For a long time it has been known that animals and plants thrive better when surrounded by an atmosphere of love – when life-promoting thoughts are focused on them. *Luther Burbank,* probably the most successful practicing botanist, consciously influenced his plants with life-promoting thoughts and achieved growth rates that had not been considered possible. Among other things, he convinced cacti – by "talking to" them – that they were safe with him and therefore could dispense with spines.

Moreover, the effect of thoughts on plants has been scientifically investigated for several decades. It has been discovered, for example, that plants react with "anxiety" to the *intention* of the experimenter to singe one of their leaves, registered with agitated movements on the measuring instruments.

The well-known biologist *Raoul France* reported that plants always respond vehemently to mental influences that are *anti-evo* and "with gratitude" to ones that are *pro-evo.*

(*Pro-evo* thoughts – with their life-promoting vibrations – noticeably improve the development of plants and animals: and *anti-evo* thoughts – with their harmful vibrations – have the opposite effect.)

See, for example, *The Secret Life of Plants* by *Peter Tompkins* and *Christopher Byrd* (Harper & Row).

(4) *What should be done in order that pro-evo objectives and modes of behavior essential for everyone will win the upper hand?*

Through enlightenment, we should motivate people to stand up for these goals and modes of behavior, non-violently but without wavering.

(5) *How can economic stability be assured even for "underdeveloped" countries that are not particularly favored with raw-material, finance or other advantages?*

In order to maintain or bring about economic stability and full employment in such a disadvantaged country, the capital invested there and the wages, salaries, fees, cash-flows and other assets created by its own efforts must remain in the country, "percolate" there – stimulating agriculture, crafts, manufacturing, construction, leisure-businesses, etc.; and capital outflows in excess of reasonable earned profits must be restricted. Capital needed to reach important economic goals should be obtained through government investment and capital investment from abroad.[42]

[42] See also "*Import-export*" under "The economy" above in this Part III.

(6) *Is there an organized network of like-minded readers of this book?*

No, but any reader who agrees with the ideas in this book can found a group of like-minded people himself or join an already existing one.

The members of such groups support one another's *pro-evo* thoughts and actions and together seek to put the ideas gained from this book into practice for the good of mankind.

(7) *Will mankind of today exterminate itself through anti-evo behavior?*

No.

Among other things, in the coming decades the development of materials and techniques and of "aids" (devices, etc.) produced therewith necessary for "artificial intelligence" will advance ever further. This development, with the help of these improved "aids", will convincingly demonstrate the unavoidable, catastrophe-prone detriments from mankind's present *anti-evo* behavior, and the many possibilities of how through *pro-evo* thinking and acting a secure and joyful future can be achieved – demonstrated so forcibly, with all detail, that the authorities and leading groups in all countries will bring about *in time* the necessary, "rescuing" changes in the behavior of mankind.

Notes

Notes

Notes

Notes

Notes

Notes

Notes

Notes

Notes